WORK REIMAGINED

**PUNCHLINE
PUBLISHERS**

MATCHPACE.NET

WORK REIMAGINED

How the power of pace can help your
organization achieve a new level of
focus, engagement, and satisfaction

ELIZABETH KNOX

with **Caitie Butler**

PUNCHLINE
PUBLISHERS

ENDORSEMENTS

Work Reimagined offers organizations and their leaders the tools to think intentionally about how they work, why they work that way, and how they can work better. This isn't just another book full of problems with no solutions: the data-driven strategies MatchPace has developed set this book apart, and readers will walk away with steps they can take today to help them work well and live well. With the world of work changing dramatically, this book is a must read for executives, managers, and employees seeking to adapt sustainably.

Jean Martin, Senior Partner, Global Head of Product,
Global Business Solutions and Career, Mercer

I personally speak to hundreds of people leaders each year—this book and the concepts are SO needed right now! Change is happening at a dizzying rate and employers are reeling from so many challenges: racial injustice, diversity and inclusion, hybrid working, post-pandemic retention, a multi-generational workforce, and so on. If organizations are to survive and thrive, they MUST explore new ways to create healthy and happy workplaces. Elizabeth expertly lays out a plan with simple tools that enable leaders to help their employees work well and live well— without sacrificing revenue and profit.

Heidi Rasmussen, Co-Founder & COO, freshbenies

My firm has adopted ideas laid out in *Work Reimagined* to help our people thrive as our organization grows. As a result, we're all better equipped to help our clients achieve their ambitious goals. If you're ready and willing to rethink how you work, the practical tools and techniques in this book will arm you to transform your organization.

Doug Hattaway, President, Hattaway Communications

When was the last time you read a management book that you couldn't put down? I had notes, exclamation points, and underlines on nearly every page of *Work Reimagined*—it's truly a playbook for exactly how to help teams work well together. We're all wrestling with what work should look like now, and this book is a powerful tool for every leader who wants to help their teams work better but doesn't know where to start.

Carrie Schum, Executive Vice President, Hattaway Communications

This book couldn't be more timely: every organization has experienced upheaval from the COVID-19 pandemic, making this the best time to reimagine a better way of working. *Work Reimagined* gives organizational leaders everything they need to navigate the future of work, helping leaders stay agile while prioritizing the wellbeing of their teams. Our organization thrived after working with MatchPace and I'm excited that everyone now has access to these powerful tools for transformation.

Rebecca Brooks, Founder and CEO, Alter Agents

We can't unleash our full potential if we're not managing our energy. *Work Reimagined* teaches organizations and individuals how to run at the right pace to empower all of us to do our best work without burning out. The strategies and tools in this book will transform you.

Molly Fletcher, author of *The Energy Clock* and *Fearless at Work*

As the founder of a certified coaching program, I know how foundational personal transformation is to any kind of organizational or systemic change. *Work Reimagined* offers a groundbreaking framework for transformation for both organizations and individuals, giving future-oriented leaders the strategies they've been missing when pursuing a better way of working.

Towanna Burrous, President of Coach Diversity Institute

Elizabeth Knox understands the need to be present for all of us to be able to do our most important work. *Work Reimagined* will help you and your team become more clear on your priorities and more willing to protect your most important asset: your attention. With intention, inspiration and inclusiveness we can set the world afire with change. Let's be present, create room to recharge and build movements together!

Terri Broussard Williams, Instructor, Social Justice Policy and Partnerships - Texas A&M, Founder of MovementMaker, Speaker, and Best Selling Author of *Find Your Fire*

Work Reimagined captivated me. As the founder of a nonprofit supporting women in the workplace and a former global executive of two Fortune 500 and one Fortune 1000 companies, I've seen firsthand how the pace at which we work keeps some of our most talented people from achieving their potential. Elizabeth and Caitie's *Work Reimagined* provides a guide for a better way for your organizations to work, giving everyone from the C-Suite on down a chance to work well without sacrificing the things that matter most to them. This book includes a very pragmatic roadmap. As I have the opportunity to mentor women in the workplace globally through 4wordwomen.org, Work Reimagined will be one of the books I recommend often.

Diane Paddison, Founder, *4word*

Work Reimagined offers HR leaders a new way of thinking about how the pace of our organizations affect the success and wellbeing of our teams. This book is full of strategies leaders can implement in their organizations right away, alongside a framework for transformation that will benefit any organization or individual who wants to work better.

Dr. Jonathan H. Westover, Chair/Professor of Organizational Leadership and Managing Partner and Principal, Human Capital Innovations

For my parents - Kathy Schloesser and Warren Schloesser. Each of you, in your own unique way, has been an example to me of working well and living well. Thank you for all you've given me. - EASK

For L and B, who I hope will one day have the chance to work in a reimagined world - CB

CONTENTS

WHY WORK MATTERS (ESPECIALLY GOOD WORK)

"How does that feel?" Sarah asked.

"Horrible!" I replied, struggling to breathe.

"How long can you keep it up?" she pressed.

"...Do I have to keep running at all?"

DURING GRADUATE SCHOOL I DID A TRIATHLON WITH my dear friends, Sarah and Laura. Conveniently, Sarah was a marathon runner, Laura was the biking expert, and I've always been a strong swimmer. We were each responsible for planning the respective workouts, pushing each other to improve in our areas of weakness.

As I was seconds from flying off the treadmill in the school gym during one of our workouts, Sarah leaned over and authoritatively pressed the "down" button so that the speed decreased from 8 MPH to 5.5 MPH. Instantly, I went from trying (and failing) to run a 7.5-minute mile to (once I caught my breath) pacing myself at a comfortable 11-minute mile.

All of a sudden, I could run for so much longer! To my shock, I didn't hate it nearly as much, either. Looking back, that moment was a key moment in helping me understand the importance of running at a healthy, sustainable pace. Best of all, I stopped hating running and had a lot more fun—not to mention, it didn't hurt so much!

When race day came, the three of us started together, got a bit separated in the swim (with poor Sarah getting a kick to the head), reconnected on the cycling leg, and finished out the run together. Training and completing the triathlon was one of the many times in my life when I learned how important it is to define success not just for myself but for a team. For us, success looked like being active, enjoying a good challenge, and, ultimately, finishing together.

That was our why—our shared goal of finishing together was more important to us than achieving any personal accomplishment. We achieved our goal by making accommodations for each other to ensure we matched pace. **The *why* drove our *how*.** Our roles were clear. We knew we had the right collective expertise for a triathlon, and we took the time to articulate who was responsible for what. We took our responsibilities seriously and functioned as a team. We had agreed on strategies to complete the race together, including how fast we were willing to go and how we would compensate for one another's weaknesses.

WHY WORKING WELL MATTERS

And what, exactly, does running a triathlon have to do with how we work? The world is full of good, hard, challenging problems that need to be solved. We need well-functioning government, well-run businesses, exemplary nonprofits, and good schools to provide real solutions to the challenges our world faces.

Our best hope for solving these problems is for people to contribute the best of their energy and efforts in the workplace. This only happens when they can sustain their attention on meaningful work and still attend to their other priorities in life (their health, family, and community). At MatchPace, we call this "working well and living well."

Our best energy and efforts are not tied to a magic number of hours in a day or by working in a particular location. You'll hear lots of "productivity gurus" promoting working a certain number of hours a day, and while we agree in theory with the concept of a shorter workday, working well is just not as simple as prescribing an optimum number of working hours for everyone, everywhere. What does matter is creating just work environments that promote people's best work, fueling their energy instead of draining it.

I believe in the cause you are fighting for, the product you are selling, the reason you exist. I know what you are doing is critical. *And I want to help you work better.*

How? **By working at a *sustainable pace*.**

One way to adjust the pace of your work is by looking at how you set your priorities, how you organize your workday, how you manage your time, and how you empower yourself and your team, so they can work well.

What you'll read in the coming chapters is how we at MatchPace help people start spending enough time working on the right things and stop spending too much time working on the wrong things. Through our work and through this book, we offer real approaches and tools that help individuals and organizations reimagine the workday to create space for collaboration and synergy, minimize the mess of a typical workday, and do the deep work that supports your mission.

You don't have to look far to see that people have tired of the nine-to-five (or eight-to-six, or seven-to-seven) grind. They feel overworked, underappreciated, and desperately lacking opportunities for creativity. You see talented people getting so frustrated with an unhealthy work-life balance that they leave their jobs to start their own companies or to take on freelance work. In the words of Daniel Pink, author of Drive, employees are ultimately searching for "autonomy, mastery, and purpose"—and they often leave their employer to find it.

I know that while new companies create amazing things, and it is great to be able to reach out and tap into experts on a freelance basis, the majority of work done today is still done by traditional organizations—small businesses, large corporations, government agencies, academic institutions, and nonprofits. To eliminate the jump-ship mentality, causing you to lose your most talented employees to something new, and also to simply help you work well so that you can accomplish your critical mission, let us help your organization *become what it needs to be* to retain your best talent *and* achieve your goals.

The way I see it, leaders have two options: They can risk their best employees burning out and leaving for an opportunity to break free from the daily grind, or organizations can break free from it themselves. It is possible to give your team the autonomy, mastery and purpose they are looking for without having to jump ship. Take your organization to a new level of focus, productivity, agility, achievement, and satisfaction by finding your own sustainable pace.

I won't tell you it's easy or hand you a quick fix. We all know those don't last. But I *will* introduce you to the life-changing concept of pace and teach you tried-and-true strategies for setting a sustainable working pace for yourself and your organization.

MatchPace exists because I care so deeply about the importance of work. That's the reason I wrote this book: to share MatchPace's best methodologies with you and your team to help you work well and live well. I promise it's one of the most worthwhile things you will pursue.

I love to work, and once I had children, I knew I couldn't parent in line with my values and be gone 50-60 hours each week. But when, as you'll see later in the book, so much of a traditional workday is wasted, should *anyone* really have to work 50-60 hours each week? Everyone has priorities outside of work that matter to them: family commitments, hobbies, taking care of their physical and mental health, places of worship, and important volunteer work. *Everyone* should have the opportunity to work well and live well.

SO WHAT IS PACE AT WORK, ANYWAY?

At MatchPace, we define pace as the **established rhythms and expectations of the workplace that enable organizations and their employees to work at a healthy, sustainable rate and accomplish their mission over the long term without burning out.**

Pace includes focus, productivity, balance, and mental health, all leading to the opposite of burnout: *sustainable effectiveness.*

Let's break this down: Pace is more than just how many hours you work in a day (though that matters). The rhythms and expectations of our workday, workweek, and work year contribute greatly to how rushed we feel at work and the amount of time and space we have to think deeply, be creative, and collaborate effectively. It doesn't matter how many or how few hours we work each day *if we're not doing the right work at the right time* to maximize our focus and productivity. Fortunately, we've developed proven methods for structuring your workday that will help you set a sustainable, effective pace.

The key word here is *sustainable.* You can be effective in the short run and still burn out if you're working in a way that isn't sustainable over the long haul. **Ultimately, you can't be truly effective if you can't sustain your effectiveness.** We all desire to do our best work over the entirety of our career because that's how we're going to experience our greatest personal and organizational success, achieve our mission, and contribute to making our world a better place. A sustainable pace will look different for every person and every organization, but discovering and pursuing sustainability is key to preventing burnout (a concept we will unpack in the following chapters).

The problem most of us face in our work is that we aren't clear on exactly what our goals are, who is responsible for what, and how we can achieve effectiveness in our work and as an organization.

Teams often don't know how to prioritize their attention. It's not clear who is supposed to do what. Some people are "running really fast" over in one area, burning themselves out, and resenting others who aren't running as fast. Others want to "run faster" but aren't sure how because they don't have clear direction or the right support. People end up expending energy on noncritical things and don't actually accomplish what they've defined as success. We think working harder or longer will get us what we want, and when that doesn't work, we try to "hack" our way to success, attempting some quick fix that is supposed to solve deeply entrenched problems.

Most of us want our organization to achieve ambitious goals well into the future. I can't think of any examples where someone started a new company or nonprofit and hoped it only lasted a year or two. But I believe success means everyone moving forward together. If you're part of a team, you need the right people around you to accomplish those goals—people who care about the same mission, have the same definition of success, and are prepared (and supported) to run at the same pace over the long haul.

Just like in my triathlon, for your organization to accomplish your own definition of success, you all want to be running together at a healthy, sustainable, *matched* pace.

If you want to take your organization further, prevent burnout, and achieve your goals, let's talk about how you can do it at the right pace. This will require digging deep into the mission, vision, and values of your organization. You'll examine norms (the unspoken and unwritten rules that dictate how your organization functions), you'll investigate whether the right people are aligned with the right responsibilities, and you'll ask yourself whether you truly have the right systems in place that support the work you're trying to do. It takes work, but this work always pays off.

On the flip side, if your organization doesn't do this work—set a healthy, sustainable pace—you'll inevitably fall short of achieving your important mission. Not to mention, when you're off pace at work, you'll likely find yourself off pace at home and in your community, leading you to underperform in all areas of your life and taking a significant toll on your physical and mental health.

Ultimately, our goal at MatchPace is to help teams *run together at a matched pace* so that you can do what you do best for the long haul. Your organization's success solves real problems facing our world today. Run too hard (work too many hours, on too many disparate projects, taking too few breaks) and you won't be able to finish the race. Everyone experiences seasons of sprinting and seasons of recovery in their career, but successful people *and* organizations look at work as a marathon— a long, steady race—so that they can achieve their mission without crashing and burning.

A ROADMAP FOR THE JOURNEY TO EFFECTIVENESS

And now we find ourselves at the starting line. Let's first review the course we'll be running together–the way this book will flow and a roadmap for our journey toward effectiveness–on our way to setting a sustainable pace at work.

In chapters 1-3, I'll share what exactly about our modern workday isn't working, and why the pace at which we work just isn't sustainable.

While it's important to understand how we got here and get a clear picture of what isn't working, our goal is to offer you solutions with MatchPace's unique lens on what it takes to create lasting change.

We believe reimagining the pace of work must be done on three different levels: as individuals, as organizations, and as a system–shown below.

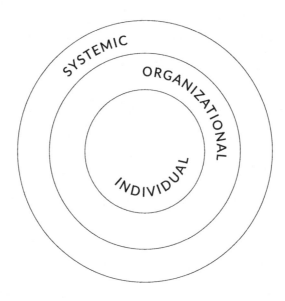

Because the primary focus of this book is helping organizations work better, I'll start there: with the center circle, Organizational Pace. In Chapters 4-7, I'll share the process we use when walking an organization toward effectiveness. While we love partnering with organizations in this process, we know that outside consultants aren't always in the budget. What we're sharing with you in this book are actual tools you can use to start implementing a sustainable pace in your own organization today.

This is our sweet spot at MatchPace: helping entire organizations discover and implement a sustainable pace that works for them. I'll begin by introducing a framework for pursuing lasting transformation and then share some tried-and-true strategies and tactics for putting pace in place in your own workplace. I'll use Chapter 7 to discuss what is quickly becoming the future of work–the hybrid workplace.

Then, together, we'll move into the innermost circle of Individual Pace in Chapters 8 and 9. This is where we'll offer one of our favorite tools for reimagining your workday: the ChronoPace. You can use this tool immediately to help you understand the unique pace at which you work best.

Once you discover your unique ChronoPace, I'll share some of my favorite strategies that I hope will help you set a sustainable pace in your own life. My aim throughout this book is to provide you with actionable strategies to move yourself toward a more sustainable pace, whatever that looks like for you. (You'll find a workbook-style Appendix in the back of this book where you can jot down answers to the exercises included throughout our journey together).

Lastly, we'll go to the outermost circle, Systemic Pace, or the pace of our systems within society and culture. In Chapter 10, we'll explore what reimagining the systems within which we work could look like to make work *work* for all of us. Our systems are the water in which we swim (or, to stick with the metaphor, the air we're all breathing as we run together). Individuals and organizations can pursue a sustainable pace, but until our systems change in a way that supports working well *and* living well, we'll be running against the pack. I encourage you to stay with us through the end, even as you start putting some of the strategies for setting a sustainable pace for yourself into action right away. The ability to reimagine work is a privilege, and until we create a society where everyone can work well and live well, our work isn't done.

I recognize I veer occasionally into slightly wonky or technical territory, but that is on purpose. I didn't want to just talk about how great it would be if we could reimagine the way we work. I want to show you *how* to work differently. This book is filled with real tools you can apply in your organization or personal work, whether you're a CEO, COO, HR leader, in middle management, or just starting your career. Use this book as a training run for practicing a sustainable pace by taking it one chapter at a time. I promise the end result is worth it!

So, just like Sarah, and Laura, and I in our triathlon, let's do this together...

CHAPTER 1

OUR MODERN WORKDAY ISN'T WORKING

After completing my Masters in Public Administration at Syracuse University (MPA—like an MBA but for government or nonprofits), I realized quickly that there weren't a lot of places for me to exercise my strengths in entry-level positions. I'm a really good project manager—I know how to understand the parts and pieces of a project and assign them to the right people to get them done. I'm good at helping other people realize and reach their potential. I'm a strong translator between people, helping others understand each other and reach their common goals.

I worked in the Intelligence Community and was instead assigned to a Subject Matter Expert-type position. Sitting alone in my cube, doing deep research into one topic and piecing together disparate pieces of information was just not my thing. I burned out from being overworked and underutilized—something that happens to people when they're working a lot, and not on the right things. In this case, it was not the right position for my skill set.

My solution to my own problem? Go into management consulting. Now I was using my skill set: I was helping people solve problems, gain insight, and make critical decisions. But I still burned out, just for different reasons. Consulting is a notoriously fast-paced field, and the stress and schedule did a number on me.

I found an "interim" job to catch my breath and recover from two different roles that had resulted in burnout. I ended up working as a financial manager for seven years, managing a $50M budget for a federal client. I did this not because the role was in my skill set or even area of interest but because the job allowed me to work from only 9-to-5, with a lot of flexibility. I had my evenings and weekends free to focus on my new marriage and other things that mattered to me: I wrote and published a book, my spouse and I renovated our house to make it net-zero (produce more energy than we consume), and we had four children. During much of that time, I worked "part-time" (intentionally in quotes).

The truth is, even when I worked full-time, I spent a whole lot of time at work not actually working—or at least not working on critical things. Beyond casual conversations with colleagues, which are important for relationship building and professional rapport, my day was often filled with a lot of talking just to make me look busy. And don't get me started on #slack and IM and email! My hours were full-time, and it was a "big" job, but I knew I was being productive for only part of the time.

When I had children, I went from air quotes "part-time" to *actual* part-time—I was supposed to only work eight hours a day, three days a week. But even though my hours decreased at work, I essentially still did the same full-time job. I quickly learned that I could complete most of the same responsibilities in those reduced hours without the distractions that often fill an eight-hour day.

Now, I've always had a reputation for being a productive person, but I knew I wasn't the only one who felt like their workday had a fair amount of chaff in it. This led me to ask the question: **Why do we use time to measure our work?**

It makes sense in a factory where production directly correlates to time. But even factory owners know you can't work nonstop and expect good outcomes. Back in the early 1900s, factory owners realized that the longer they kept factories open, the more mistakes workers made. They concluded (with the pressure of organized labor) that longer hours led to subpar results.

Similarly, spending more time doing a knowledge-based job does not produce more. In fact, it can lead to diminishing marginal returns. Our brains don't think faster or more creatively over longer hours—they just get tired. We lose focus and we start making mistakes. It's hard to be creative and come up with quality ideas that actually solve problems when we're working hour after hour with fractured attention.

Our workweeks are simply too long, due to both the unreasonable expectations about availability in our 24-7 connected world and our unwillingness to separate "time spent working" from performance metrics. I believe the latter is the crux of the problem: When we measure how effective we are at work by our long slog through the workday (and into evenings and weekends) instead of by *outcomes*, we set ourselves up for both ineffectiveness and burnout.

QUANTITY ≠ QUALITY

Studies show that the average knowledge-based worker completes about two hours and twenty-three minutes of productive work in a day.[1] The rest of the workday is filled up with organizing their work (important, but not worth five hours of the day), questionably necessary meetings and mountains of email—things that make us *look* busy but aren't helping us produce much of anything. And the truth is, those 2.5+ hours of work are not far off from what brain science says we can actually do.

We think we should be able to do 40 or more hours of productive work each week, but we really can't. Studies have shown our concentration wanes the longer we're at work.[2] We become less efficient, taking more time to make decisions and losing sharpness. As the hours tick away, we experience the law of diminishing returns: we take longer to get work done and often end up with lower-quality outputs.

People *are* putting in long hours—I believe people when they say they're putting in 50-60 hours or more at work each week. But how many of those hours are producing quality work? Those hours may feel like "hard work," but are they filled with the *right* work?

Plus, when we're putting in those long hours, we're often working on more than one thing at a time—multitasking—which is a productivity and creativity killer. When we're interrupted at work, it can take minutes or longer to recover our attention to what we were originally working on— 15-plus minutes to get back to what you were doing, according to Dr. Gloria Mark at UC Irvine[3] (more on this in Chapter 3). In fact, when we think we're multitasking, we're actually task-switching: moving back and forth between two unrelated tasks, which does a major number on our ability to do anything well.[4]

Inspiration and new ideas aren't tied to particular hours. Our brains get tired. Just because we're committed to punching the clock for a set number of hours a day doesn't mean those hours are fertile for creativity and productivity. We need to design our workdays to maximize our brain power, reduce distractions and interruptions, discourage multitasking, and truly structure the workday to get work done. It turns out, those 2.5 hours a day we actually spend doing productive work isn't that far off from the number of hours our brain is actually able to do good work!

OFF THE CLOCK ≠ REST

Another challenge with our modern workday is that our 24/7, increasingly connected, "always on" economy does more harm than good. We've bought into the lie that we have to work longer, faster, and harder to get ahead. Maybe we've even convinced ourselves we're working so hard for the greater good—that the only way to achieve the purpose we've been created for is to burn ourselves out along the way.

If our lives are so wrapped up in our work and the way working makes us feel that we're uncomfortable simply existing for a few days at a time *without* working (or checking email or endlessly scrolling), we're in deep trouble. Jon Staff and Pete Davis, owners of the tiny house rental company Getaway, discuss the cure for overwork in their book, *How to Get Away.* They explain that "experiencing real leisure requires being in an environment that allows you to cease effort and analysis, performance and criticism, bustle and worry."[5] When we derive our purpose and meaning entirely from effort, performance, and hustle, we don't just burnout; we sacrifice some of the most important things in life: our relationships, spirituality, and presence in our communities.

And "fake rest" doesn't count, either. We interviewed Pete for MatchPace's *You Need To Stop Doing That* podcast. During our conversation, Pete argued that too often those in the knowledge worker class pretend to be doing restful leisure activities, but in reality, they are just filling their time with other types of productivity and not truly restful activities, until they can start working again. Some of those activities are even work posing as rest, like reading books that we think will enhance our professional performance. Just because you're reading that productivity guru's book in your "downtime" doesn't mean it's truly restful and restorative.

OVERWORK ≠ QUALITY WORK

Our physical work environments may have improved since the Industrial Age days of factory work, but these long workweeks are still taking a significant toll on our health.

Consider these statistics:

- 23% of full-time employees say they feel burned out at work *very often or always*, with another 44% feeling sometimes burned out

- Burnout at work leads to an estimated $125 to $190 *billion* in health care spending every year

- Employees who are burned out are more likely to experience type 2 diabetes, coronary heart disease, gastrointestinal issues, depression, high cholesterol and even death before the age of 45

- As many as *one million people* in the United States miss work each day because of stress, translating to a loss of $150 to $300 billion for employers each year[6]

Let's do a quick pop quiz. If you totaled up all the hours you spent working this past week—not just hours you were sitting in your office (at work or at home), but phone calls you took during your commute, emails you checked and answered first thing in the morning or late at night, or work you did after the kids were in bed—how many hours did you *really* spend working?

If you're like the average American knowledge worker, the answer is probably beyond the assumed "40-hour workweek." But how many of those were valuable hours, creating real change—not just shuffling email around and checking newsfeeds? How many times did you have meetings sprinkled throughout your day, giving you just enough time to do nothing of real value in between? How many times did you only have one or two tasks to do, but you put them off till the end of the day so at least you knew you had something to do?

We thought technology would make our lives easier and offer us shorter workweeks, but in this Post-Industrial Age, we're working more than ever before: an average of 47 hours per week,[7] in fact. This is nearly a 20% increase over the traditional 9-to-5 workday. And 18% of Americans consistently clock 60 or more hours of work every week.

It's time to change the way we work. Overwork causes inability to focus and then burnout, which frequently leads to low job satisfaction, poor workplace morale, and, subsequently, high turnover rates.

This was true for one mission-driven nonprofit we consulted with. Employees were stressed over unclear expectations and scope, resulting in all of the above-mentioned issues. At an organizational level we identified a revolving door of team members, costing the nonprofit more in training, loss of institutional knowledge, and concern from donors. One staff member was so affected, it led to a mental health crisis that landed them in the hospital! That may be an extreme example, and other factors likely contributed to unhealthy stress levels, but there was no doubt that work-related stress was a factor.

Everyone experiences work stress at different points in their career: a tight deadline, job searching, a colleague's family emergency that causes a crunch for you at work. But too often, the way we're working is the problem.

What if working 40, 50, or 60 hour weeks, as many do (and as is normal in our culture), is hurting our ability to achieve our purpose at work? We've been metaphorically running in an all-out sprint for so long that we're at risk of collapsing—if we haven't already.

OUTCOME-FOCUSED WORK

At this point, you may be saying to yourself, "I've *tried* to stop working so much, but I just can't seem to slow down. Is it even possible to stop overworking?" The answer is, thankfully, *yes*–but it's not easy. And eliminating unnecessary overwork requires organizational change as much as a personal commitment to a sustainable working pace.

We inherited a way of managing employees from the Industrial Age, when productivity was measured by how many units a worker could produce in a set number of hours. This is called "managing to time," and managing this way just doesn't make sense in a knowledge economy.

As the U.S. entered the Industrial Age, workers began to transition to a regimented workday. Later, factory owners started implementing a 5-day workweek and reduced the workday—what we now call the 9-to-5—in the 1920s. Then, along came service and information jobs in the 1950s and 60s. But we still structured our workday as if we were working in factories. People were still managed by the number of hours worked, even though we all know that time spent at work does not guarantee anything is actually produced.

Over 60 years later, we're still using an Industrial Age framework to determine how we should work. Our current workdays are a mishmash of too many meetings, management by email, and constant interruptions. Plus, they're just too long to effectively focus all day. Our outdated and inefficient workdays simply stretch longer than our available brain power.

The solution?

Outcome-focused work.

It's hard to rewire our brains and organizations to think differently about how we measure our success at work on any given day. But the shift is relatively simple: Instead of starting your workday thinking, "I just need to get through until five o'clock, and then I can head home," begin by asking yourself, "What do I need to accomplish today to move us forward in our organizational mission?" Then, you figure out what activities are required to accomplish those daily tasks–meetings, times for collaboration, or times for deep focus (more on that next). Once you've achieved your outcomes for the day and supported your colleagues where they needed help to accomplish theirs, you're free to go home, whether at five p.m. or one p.m. In an ideal world, you'd have completed your work, delivered the value your organization is paying you for, and can leave. But most organizations aren't culturally ready for that shift.

Managing outcomes instead of time gives you your time back. Managing outcomes is both the solution to overwork and the secret to not just freedom of time but the freedom to focus, be more creative, and feel satisfied in your work.

In the transition away from managing time toward managing outcomes, managers often feel a temporary loss of control as they adjust to thinking differently about the workday. Yes, it's easier in some ways to require employees to be in their office working between a certain set of hours, but you end up paying people to sit in place for a set amount of time without guaranteeing they're producing more while sitting there.

Instead, outcome-focused work rewards work produced instead of time spent at work, whether those hours were actually productive or not. This incentivizes employees to focus, optimize their productivity, and achieve quality outcomes—even or especially if they can do it in less than eight hours a day—giving them their time back. The result? More focused, productive employees who are less burned out, more committed to your mission, and healthier mentally and physically.

Our greatest desire for our workplaces is that we remember they are made up of human beings and that a workplace without humanity isn't a workplace worth working at. Outcome-focused work is a critical part of restoring humanity to our workplace.

There is some work involved to understand how to determine which outcomes you need to focus on, and our holistic approach will help you figure that out. Let's keep going!

CHAPTER 2

REIMAGINING THE WORKDAY

THINK SOME OF THE GROWING PAINS I HAD EARLY ON IN my career were just that—growing pains. I was trying different things on, seeing what fit, finding out what didn't. I ping-ponged between "bored at work but with social bandwidth" in one professional environment, to "professional engagement but no time for other activities" in another. Where was the "professionally engaged AND having time for other priorities" type of job? And that question I had about why we use time-based measurements of productivity and accomplishment remained unanswered.

The truth was and still is: I *love* to work—on meaningful work. I love how organizations provide solutions to our collective global problems as well as people's individual problems. I love how we can provide real answers to real questions through our work. I love how the wages people earn at organizations help them take care of their families. I love how they make our world a better place.

I know I'm not the only one who wants to make a deep contribution to the world through my professional work and be deeply connected to my family, friends, and community. And I don't think that's too much to ask for.

It's because of my love for that kind of meaningful work that MatchPace came to be. I want organizations to function better. I want people aligned in the right jobs, doing the right work, with the right focus so that people can both *work well and live well*. At MatchPace, we call this process *reimagining your workday*.

When I started MatchPace, I was (perhaps overly) optimistic about the amount of time it takes for organizations to implement lasting change. I didn't even know there was a whole discipline called organizational design (OD), with experts who had been working through these challenges for decades. I'm glad I didn't know—I don't think I would have been as quick to start a company if I realized there were already so many experts in the field! But I absolutely believe that we offer a unique lens on OD that we all need. **Our aim is to help organizations redesign themselves to accomplish their mission, improve workplace engagement, and give people back their energy, attention, and time.**

We learned in our first year that reimagining the workday is way more complicated than simply telling people to stop wasting their attention or to try shortening the workday. For one thing, you can only successfully shorten the workday after you've made some other significant adjustments to the way you work. And there is a lot to do to make the workplace more effective (and thereby more productive, more enjoyable, and more satisfying) other than just shortening the workday. We **truly** want to give people back their time, and there are a lot of other benefits we've brought to organizations, too.

We put this lesson into practice when we engaged with a small-but-mighty marketing agency. A few months into the COVID-19 pandemic, they started to notice increasing levels of burnout on their team. They'd heard about the four-day workweek and were curious about implementing a shorter workweek as a way to provide some much-needed relief to their team.

As they piloted a shorter workweek, they realized it was actually causing them *more* stress. While we think a four-day workweek can be a great tool to minimize overwork, this organization still needed to do the deeper work of shifting to outcome-focused work and putting strategies in place to help their team focus and collaborate more effectively on the days they were working.

So, we helped them step back, evaluate the source of their burnout, and find a solution that enabled them to continue to provide service excellence to their clients, as well as reduce the stress level of the team. There is no "one size fits all" solution to overwork, burnout and ineffectiveness. By focusing on the pace at which their organization needed to work to work well sustainably, they found a solution that worked for them.

At the core of our work is *attention*. It's not time management or energy hacks. It's realizing that what gets most of your attention during the workday often isn't what you need to be doing to achieve your goals and objectives. This leaves you overworked, burned out, and feeling like you're never caught up.

I had a coaching client who was frustrated that her boss emailed her at night. She said she never responded because she didn't want him to think she was available after hours. I asked why she looked at her email after work if she didn't plan on responding. Her response was it was only a few minutes and she liked to have an idea of what was going on so she was prepared the next day. Then, I asked if that really only took a few minutes of her time. And the realization hit: She wasn't giving her boss the three minutes of time that it took to scan her inbox—she was giving her boss *her whole evening*.

By simply scanning her inbox a few times each night, she'd stew and steam that he'd emailed or think through what he'd emailed about. She didn't spend just a few minutes looking at her email, but gave all of her evening's attention to whatever her inbox held. (It should be said that once she had a conversation with her boss, she learned he did not expect her to respond or even check her email at night—an important "norm" we will talk about in Chapter 6.)

Does any of this sound familiar?

- Having time to work but allowing meetings to get splattered all over your day

- Knowing that the number of hours you've worked doesn't dictate the quality of solutions you produce

- Never really giving yourself uninterrupted time to allow creativity to bubble up

- Wanting so badly to help people, but having too many priorities to actually work on any of them effectively

This is what happens when we work too many hours *on the wrong things*. They make our days too long, cause brain fog, heighten our stress, and hurt our relationships at work and presence at home. These frustrations are familiar to almost all of us. And the reality is, even the best time management techniques won't work unless you also manage your attention.

Attention span refers to the amount of time an individual can remain focused on a task without becoming distracted. This is an important variable since people with longer attention spans are able to be more creative, make fewer errors, and are more likely to achieve their goals. Current researchers argue that the average attention span of American adults has dropped and is limited to 20, 10, or even five minutes. We need more than five minutes at a time to provide quality work. How did we get here?

The number of things competing for our attention has drastically increased and has trained us for a "newness bias." We're looking for the next shiny object—be it refreshing our inbox, "pulling down the slot" of social media (yes, it was designed to resemble the feel of a slot machine), or a new project that will hopefully have a groundbreaking outcome. We're constantly hoping for some new news.

While the dopamine hit we get with something new may feel good, it's not helpful for the *deep work* needed to create *meaningful work*.

This is at the root of what we do at MatchPace. We help people and organizations be honest about what really requires their attention (and be honest with themselves about where their attention actually is). When our clients learn how to apply and sustain focus on the right things at the right pace, the magic happens in their organizations.

Could solving our problems of burnout, overwork, and poor work-life balance—all of which lead to poor outcomes for your organization—really be addressed with the power of the right pace? We think so, and we will show you how.

TELEWORK AND FLEXTIME ≠ SILVER BULLET

At this point, you may be thinking, "So is the solution to chronic overwork and an unsustainable working pace just letting everyone work from home?" While telecommuting and flex schedules may work for some employees at some organizations and are considerably more common now than they were before the COVID-19 pandemic, a "matched pace" is still really important for an organization regardless of where their employees are located. In Chapters 6 and 7, we'll introduce you to the concepts of Core Hours and Hybrid Work, two tools to give employees the flexibility and autonomy they need to work at a sustainable pace whether they're physically in the office, working from home, or traveling.

Working in person leads to a level of synergy that is difficult to replicate virtually, except with special and often long-standing relationships. For most people, the good collaboration that happens in person accelerates creativity, new ideas, and solutions, helping them get unstuck faster. The primary problems with our workday aren't due to where people are working from but instead how they are working—this includes clear priorities and workdays structured for optimal effectiveness. If we don't eliminate the unnecessary distractions ((like a mess of meetings with no time to focus), those distractions and unhelpful norms will persist whether we operate in person or virtually.

There are other challenges with remote work and flex schedules, too. If everyone is flexing at different times, it's hard to get the answers you need when you need them, and your message or email may go unanswered for hours or days. Had you been in the same place—caught one another a few minutes before or after a meeting, in the hallway, or perhaps in the break room—you could have had your question answered in minutes instead of days.

Unless you shift to managing outcomes instead of time, the same issues with overwhelm and burnout follow you wherever you go. While remote work will likely become increasingly common and offer many added benefits, it also brings its own set of challenges and preconceived notions. There is a reason people give air quotes to "telework". There has historically been an assumption that working outside of the office isn't *really* working.

That perception is changing now that so many organizations have shifted to remote or hybrid work, but miscommunication still occurs. For example, perceptions between coworkers about others' level of effort can lead to deteriorating working relationships and interpersonal conflict. Similarly, telework and flextime are often treated as benefits, given as a "favor" to employees, instead of viewed as a way to meet the real challenge of helping them work at a sustainable pace.

While telework is an increasingly popular way of working, there are some times when it doesn't work. Two instances where it concerns me are when it impacts your ability to accomplish your organization's mission and when it's a cover for disengagement (and sometimes both of those things at the same time). An organization we consulted with shared that all of their employees wanted to continue working exclusively remotely as the COVID-19 pandemic ended. However, they are an organization that provides a direct service to their community. Not being present (at all) with the people they were helping was eventually going to lead to a decrease in effectiveness. The deeper we dug, we saw that the organization was facing pretty significant employee disengagement. And when we dug even deeper than that, we saw that the employee disengagement was a result of other fundamental problems at the organization—a lack of clarity around the vision and the roles and responsibilities of team members and a lack of trust among team members. Telework, when not additive to the mission or when used to avoid addressing underlying problems, only serves to detract from effectiveness.

Ultimately, *where* your organization works is less important than *how* they are working. Remote and flexible work can help, but are far from a silver bullet and require thoughtfulness to make sure they are implemented well. Then, organizations can successfully help everyone work at a healthy, sustainable pace.

DEEP WORK

We've referenced the concept of deep work a few times now, and deep work is a critical component of achieving your goals and experiencing satisfaction at work. But our workday, our technology, and our culture make deep work really hard. Deep work, a concept coined by author and computer science professor Cal Newport, is:

> "Professional activity performed in a state of distraction-free concentration that pushes your cognitive capabilities to their limit. These efforts create new value, improve your skill, and are hard to replicate."

Sounds great, right? But if you've tried setting aside time to focus and struggle to sustain deep work for more than a few minutes, you're not alone.

Sometimes it helps to define something by what it is not in order to understand what it is. The opposite of deep work is "shallow work":

> "Noncognitively demanding, logistical-style tasks, often performed while distracted. These efforts tend not to create much new value in the world and are easy to replicate."[8]

So what does *that* mean? Unfortunately, the word "shallow" is a bit of a dismissive misnomer. Shallow work consists of administrative functions that *have* to be done for an organization to function and run well. In this case, shallow does not mean unimportant or not valuable. Another [imperfect] way to describe these tasks and functions is "hygiene." Flossing your teeth isn't fun, glamorous, or the type of obvious task that invites praise, but you have to do it to prevent cavities. It simply keeps your mouth healthy.

The workday equivalent of flossing are tasks that seem boring, like articulating how people should use travel time, giving annual reviews, or making the effort to run more effective and efficient meetings. If you don't do them, your proverbial teeth fall out. And you need your teeth (both literal and figurative) at work.

If you don't maintain proper workplace hygiene, you'll spend far more time "at the dentist" trying to manage your work (remember, in most organizations over 60% of the average workday is spent just managing work, not doing it), and you end up with burned-out team members, miscommunication, unclear expectations, and high turnover. The stakes are high if you neglect this "shallow" work.

It seems like half of our work at MatchPace exists because our clients don't value shallow work or give it the priority it needs. Many of our client organizations were started by visionaries who sometimes forget the importance of operations. The other half of our work exists because our clients end up trying to do deep work in a shallow way. Their workdays are so fragmented that they find themselves trying to write important reports in 10-minute snippets between checking email and half-listening in a meeting. They're left with a shoddy report, an ineffective meeting, and inefficient emails that end up taking more of your time.

This is the way most of us work at work. But it isn't working. We We need to pay attention to the work of running our organizations. We don't expect any other relationship or system to keep going without attention and maintenance. And, a knowledge economy requires deep work in order to add value at our jobs and to society. We need time to think—ot just in snippets—without interruptions and distractions. Time that allows us to truly focus, wrestle with ideas, and be inspired—not just regurgitate the same old ideas. Deep work is the only way to truly discover solutions that move the ball forward and help us stay on pace. Deep work is how we'll solve the real problems facing our world today.

CHAPTER 3

THE RISK IN RUNNING OFF PACE

When considering the importance of pace, it might help to think about what happens when you're *off pace*. Let's return to the running metaphor: Say you have a personal goal of running a 5K in 25 minutes. That means you need to average about an eight-minute mile over the course of your run (which, as noted above, wouldn't be my goal!). If you pace yourself at a ten-minute mile, well, you're just not going to hit your goal. If you sprint the first two miles, you'll tire too quickly or even injure yourself and still fall short of that 25-minute goal.

A much better approach is to find your eight-minute-mile stride and stick with it over the course of the race, finishing right on time—without collapsing before the finish line.

Remember my initially miserable running experience as I was training for the triathlon? If I hadn't paced myself appropriately, one of two things would have happened: I would have injured myself, burned out, and given up, or I would have gotten bored. Pacing allowed me to both take care of my body *and* achieve my stated mission. Oh, and it was a lot more enjoyable, too!

If you've ever run or watched a long-distance race, you know there are "pacers" that act as a guide for runners, running at different paces to help racers know just how fast they're going. If you know your optimal pace is an eight-minute mile, you find that pacer and stick close to them throughout the race. If you fall behind, you may have to sprint at the end, but you'll still be aware of your pace and closer to achieving your goal.

The exact same is true at work. If you outline your goals for the year, but your workday doesn't give you the ability to focus and achieve important milestones along the way, you're going to finish the year falling short of your goals. Likewise, if you take on too much work and try to sustain extra-long workweeks, over the course of the year, you're likely to get overstressed, burned out and sick, leaving you unable to finish the year strong. Both scenarios are equally unfortunate; but luckily, they're equally preventable if you can sustain the right pace.

Sadly, most of the "focus hacks" found on blogs and in articles don't make a dent in our ability to focus at work. That's because our workdays and workspaces aren't designed to facilitate focus. This is why the majority of MatchPace's work focuses on helping organizations change, rather than prioritizing individuals. Because it doesn't matter if you know how to do deep work; if you're in an organization that doesn't value it or make it possible, it won't do you a whole lot of good during your workday. We will give you strategies to set a sustainable pace personally, but unless your organization aims for a sustainable pace, you'll find yourself stymied at every turn.

Imagine trying to do deep work in the middle of Hartsfield—Jackson Atlanta International Airport—not possible, right? While our workplaces (hopefully) aren't as chaotic as America's busiest airport, supposed developments like instant message and open offices make it feel like we're working at a busy intersection and certainly make it more difficult to focus and produce quality work.

It turns out, weeks and years of struggling to focus, feeling repeatedly unable to accomplish both major and minor tasks, and working into evenings and on weekends takes a toll. Society has a name for what happens when you're running off pace, working too long and too hard without the autonomy to focus, get creative, and maximize effectiveness. It's a word we're all familiar with: **burnout.**

Burnout is much more than a buzzword. It's a lived experience for hundreds of thousands of American workers that impacts not just their work life but also their personal lives. Burnout has become so pervasive, it's a syndrome acknowledged by the World Health Organization (WHO). In the most recent International Classification of Diseases, the WHO, for the first time, included burnout as a syndrome with its very own code, enabling healthcare professionals to properly diagnose and treat it. According to WHO, "Burn-out is a syndrome conceptualized as resulting from chronic workplace stress that has not been successfully managed. It is characterized by three dimensions: 1) feelings of energy depletion or exhaustion; 2) increased mental distance from one's job, or feelings of negativism or cynicism related to one's job; and 3) reduced professional efficacy."[9]

When Burnout Syndrome was first coined in the 1970s, it was defined as a "psychological syndrome emerging as a prolonged response to chronic interpersonal stressors on the job, [resulting in] an overwhelming exhaustion, feelings of cynicism and detachment from the job, and a sense of ineffectiveness and lack of accomplishment."[10]

According to research conducted at UC Berkeley, 28% of working Americans self-identify that they are facing burnout as we speak; that number jumps to over 60% if you include those who don't self-identify as burned out but exhibit the same signs and symptoms, including:

- Exhaustion
- Cynicism and detachment
- Sense of ineffectiveness
- Anger
- Insomnia
- Substance abuse and addiction
- Depersonalization of others (often coworkers)
- Physical illness[11]

Burnout leaves employees 63% more likely to take a sick day, 23% more likely to visit the emergency room, and over twice as likely to leave their job when they otherwise would have stayed. They are also 2.6 times as likely to be actively seeking a different job.[12] That means burnout has real consequences for organizations, not just individuals.

Are you scared yet? Burnout Syndrome is real, and it cripples us at work—not to mention in our personal lives. Burnout in one area of our lives simply feeds into others.

This phenomenon has been named the "Spillover Effect," which occurs when difficulties at work cause undue stress and tension in relationships at home. Spillover from a stressful work environment can lead to an increase in arguments between spouses or withdrawing emotionally from partners and children. Heightened stress at home then spills back into our work lives, triggering a downward cycle that hurts an employee's ability to focus and produce high-quality work (at best) and leads to further deteriorating home relationships (at worst).

For people who deeply love their work, I believe you should not and do not have to make a choice between professional success and physical, emotional, and relational health. It doesn't have to be either-or.

But how? Is it really possible to unwind an organizational ball of chaos and create a work environment that gives employees clarity, protects against scope creep, rewards effectiveness, and gives people back their time while still finding meaning in their work?

Long story short, burnout is real and it really affects our physical, mental, and emotional health, not to mention our ability to do our job. None of us wants to experience "reduced professional efficacy," but as many as two-thirds of us can thank burnout for preventing us from doing our jobs well.

Is there hope? Yes! Burnout can be solved—or even prevented—with the power of pace.

GETTING ON PACE

As our working hours tick away, we experience the law of diminishing returns: We take longer to get work done, and often end up with a lower quality work product.[13] That means those last three, four, or even more hours of your workday are probably not having the impact you're hoping for.

Multitasking and endless interruptions contribute to the law of diminishing returns. Dr. Gloria Mark of the University of California found that knowledge workers are interrupted nearly every three minutes, and it takes 15 minutes to refocus after an interruption.[14] Did you catch that? Knowledge workers are interrupted nearly 20 times an hour, and it takes them 15 minutes to refocus. Why is this important? Because if we're never allowed extended time—even an hour—to focus on deep work, we either don't move the ball forward, or we move it forward s-l-o-o-o-o-w-l-y.

Forcing our brains to work beyond their capacity and subjecting them to constant interruptions like they are open tabs in your browser is problematic, especially as brain fatigue can contribute to making mistakes and, of course, burning out. One study revealed managers couldn't tell the difference in output and performance between an employee who works

80 hours per week and one who just pretends to.[15] And overwork hurts employees by leading to higher stress levels and health problems, which, in turn, hurts an organization's bottom line.[16] Expecting employees to work excessively long hours or be "always on" is a lose-lose scenario.

If the way we're working isn't working for our brains, how can organizations apply the science behind how our brains work to help set a sustainable working pace?

I know it takes guts to reimagine the workday–especially by shortening it–but many organizations are realizing a workday as short as six, five or even four hours gives employees the motivation to get their work done while allowing them the freedom to invest in other priorities. This makes for more productive working hours and a healthier, happier team. Not ready to take that step? Get serious about an *only* eight-hour workday, and put organizational norms in place that prevent work from creeping into evening and weekend hours (more on how to do that soon).

Regardless of workday length, organizations need to **establish time** *during the actual workday* **for deep focus and creative collaboration**. Most people do their best work at the start of their day, so allow employees a few hours in the morning for uninterrupted deep work. Then, allot time in the afternoon for meetings, allowing brains tired from focused effort to refresh through creative collaboration.

Now that we've spent some time exploring the context for why our workday is the way it is and why we need more than "quick fixes" to achieve a sustainable pace at work, let's revisit our roadmap. Next on our journey, I'll introduce a framework to unpack what lasting transformation in our organizations and ourselves requires. Then, I'll talk about how to actually do that deeper work, first as an organization, then as individuals, and finally as society as a whole. I don't claim it will be easy, but I promise it's worth it.

CHAPTER 4

WORK^POWER

W HEN MATCHPACE FIRST ENGAGES WITH A NEW
client, they usually want a relatively quick
deliverable to demonstrate the return on their investment. I get it. It's a
financial, time, and even emotional sacrifice to pursue organizational change
and effectiveness. But even if you make all the changes in the world to your
workday, workplace policies, or the management tools you use, nothing will
stick without deeper transformation.

At MatchPace, we prioritize organizational change because we know it is
crucial for the organization to accomplish their mission, and we understand
the individual hardship felt when one's time, effort, and attention is wasted at
work. That's why we're starting in our second concentric circle: Organizational
Pace. We understand the compounded frustration of continually operating
within a work structure that is blind to that waste. Without change at the
organizational level, any improvements an individual may make to how they
work won't go far and certainly won't last. Without organizational-level

change, burnout becomes inevitable, regardless of how creative, passionate, or talented team members are. Without organizational-level change, there just can't be lasting, sustainable change.

And organizational change only happens when individuals decide it's time to change the organization. This is where the two inner circles from the concentric circle actually become like an infinity sign for change: The only way an organization can change is when individuals within that organization decide it's time to change the system, and the only way an individual can change is if they're in an organization that supports that change. We simply cannot strong arm anyone into true change. A team has to be willing to get out of their comfort zone and do the deeper work of examining how they're working, why they're working that way, and why it isn't working. Surface-level change doesn't last.

This is where our Work^Power [read: "*Work to the Power*"] framework comes in.

WORK¹   WORK²   WORK³

When we engage with a client, we know there are three layers of work we have to address: what we call Work to the Power (Work^Power). Take the example of painting a room. We all know there's more than meets the eye with any task, and a painting project is no exception. We'll use this metaphor to help break down the different layers of Work^Power.

Consider the physical act of putting paint on walls. At first glance, this may seem like the only deliverable—the end goal (Work^1). But in order to get a room painted, especially painted correctly, there's also the work of prepping the room: moving furniture, laying down drop cloths, taping trim, etc. It's a lot of work to paint a room, so knowing *why* you're painting it and having a vision for the finished product is key to carrying you through all the steps it takes, from prep work to final coat (Work^2).

Even deeper than the preparation is the work of thinking about what feeling you want your room to have. How will this new paint color help create an environment that fits your lifestyle and your personality? How will it encourage the type of mood you want people to feel when they enter that room? Are you hoping to create a calm, zen space that encourages rest? Or a bright, cheery space that facilitates conversation or sparks creativity? All are valid. But without thinking through this step (Work^3), you might end up with an end product that looks okay but doesn't actually accomplish what you'd set out to accomplish. Now, let's unpack the metaphor a bit more...

WORK^1

As with painting a room, the work we do is similarly layered. The first layer of work we provide to the client is what we call Work^1 ("Work to the First Power"). Through careful consultation, assessments, and exercises, many of which I'll share with you as you read further, MatchPace determines the customized deliverables. Maybe our client needs a new set of roles and responsibilities, or they want to develop a training program. Work^1 deliverables satisfy the on-paper needs of the client, at least on the surface.

WORK^2

Work^2 ("Work to the Second Power"—you get the idea!) is the actual change that happens in an organization as a result of implementing Work^1. It's when the group starts thinking about things differently, shifting the *tone* of the organization. When a team begins to understand the wins behind the new changes, they are more likely to sustain those changes. Conversely, without this greater understanding, a team will try out a new way of working for a few weeks and then fall back into old habits and patterns because they don't see how those changes support their larger mission. Sound familiar?

To continue our painting metaphor, consider two partners who agree that they want to paint their living room white to make it a bright and open space. They've decided they want to create an atmosphere for gathering friends together and inspire meaningful conversation and relaxation. If they keep this goal in mind as they begin to prepare and paint their room, when they hit an inevitable snag, like requiring an extra coat of paint, or are just burned out and ready for the project to be done, that shared vision keeps them going. They may even discover areas of miscommunication to address through the course of their project. Without a goal or purpose in mind, the project might have felt like just one more chore to be done or been a cause of tension in the relationship. Instead, their shared goal and understanding shapes the tone of the whole project and carries them through.

This deeper, often interpersonal work is the crux of Work^2.

WORK^3

Work^3 is the personal transformation that can happen as a result of Work^1 and Work^2. It's when an individual realizes their own patterns and behaviors that haven't been serving them. They begin to identify personal actions that have been getting in the way of their own objectives or the objectives of the organization. This final shift in thinking makes accomplishing Work^1 and Work^2 that much more lasting and effective.

Painting a room has *some* value—it's a finished product—but unless you did the deeper work, it's *just* a finished product. Pretty much anyone can slap some paint on the walls (or, for a more work-related analogy, write up a document about roles and responsibilities). But at the very least, you want someone to have the foresight to remember to tape up the trim, cover furniture, and patch any holes (get the organization to think about how they work together and what the new roles actually mean). And particularly if you're pursuing a painting project with a partner or a team, the better your self-awareness and ability to communicate, the smoother the project will go (helping people realize the work they need to do to grow into the role they are meant to fulfill on a team).

But it takes deep thoughtfulness and intention to paint a room in a way that invites the feeling you want to experience in that room. It takes a larger vision for the design of your home to end up with a cohesive aesthetic. And while there are times when you just need paint on the wall, most of the time, you are trying to create an environment that fits your style and needs. In the workplace, this means coming to a deep understanding of *your* role, how your previous behavior was standing in the way of yourself and your colleagues, and what you need to do to change your perspectives, attitudes, and behaviors. Work^3 doesn't just help organizations work better; it helps them work better *together*.

More often than not, clients hire us thinking they want Work^1. They want clarity on their roles and responsibilities, or they want a new schedule that makes space for both collaboration and focus. But where we really strive to deliver value is in Work^2 and Work^3. That's where the meaningful change takes place, and it's what sustains Work^1. Doing the work of Work^2 and Work^3 also ensures you can keep doing your best Work^1. (Because how many times have you tried implementing a new project management software or a new policy, and it doesn't stick? You need more than just a quick solution.)

If you try to change anything—any process, any policy, any framework—and you don't sift through the layers of behaviors and beliefs that get in your way, it's like putting paint on a surface that won't take. It will peel before you know it. The only way to make real change at an organization or as an individual is to assess all three layers and do the work to make that change sustainable and lasting.

Now that we've painted a picture of Work^Power (pun intended), let's take a closer look at the Work^Power framework in action.

WORK^POWER IN ACTION

MatchPace worked with an organizational client to help them sort out their knowledge management system. Hats off to this organization because most places don't invest in knowledge management (KM)—instead, they designate (often subconsciously) the person who has been there the longest to be a walking, breathing KM system. When that person leaves, all that knowledge goes with them. Or, if they do have a KM system, it sits somewhere on a drive or in an online tool without ever being used, rendering it quickly outdated and unhelpful.

In this client's case, the deliverables were pretty straightforward: project planning, deciding on a platform, creating modules of existing knowledge, and then inputting them into that system. That was Work^1. KM systems take a lot of brainstorming, planning, and implementation to ensure they will work for everyone. The client could have stopped there.

Instead, they dug deeper. From the Work^1 process, teams realized it would take ongoing, intentional effort to capture knowledge. They would need to be aware that they might need to create new modules of information after each project or periodically evaluate the system to make sure it remained useful and up-to-date. Remember when we said Work^2 is about shifting the tone of the organization because of a shared vision and purpose? By realizing their need to prioritize KM, they were able to identify their why behind consistently capturing, storing, and updating knowledge. This empowered them to become a learning organization—not stagnant or dependent on oral tradition but actively involved in capturing and transmitting knowledge. This discovery was Work^2.

Finally, the layer of Work^3. People get busy, projects pile up, and deadlines loom. What motivates busy team members to actually follow through, use their knowledge management system, and then follow through again on the next project? That's the final layer of Work^3. Every team member had to internalize the norm of information updates, as well as normalize the expectation that colleagues would do the same. They had to believe that this mode of information-sharing was crucial to the health and sustainability of the company, acknowledging that holding on to knowledge other people needed was actually hindering the company's growth.

Often, the subconscious refusal to use a KM system has a lot to do with believing you're the only person who can do something right. When every team member focuses instead on the organization's sustainability and admits there will likely be a time in the future when someone else will step into their shoes, then a knowledge management system will serve its purpose and keep the organization effective. Ultimately, organizational change comes down to personal transformation.

Do you see how important all three layers of Work^Power are? Work^1 might achieve your goal on paper, but without the other two deeper layers, you'll end up right back where you started.

And that's what we mean by the infinity loop—we work with organizations to help them create an environment where individuals can thrive, and we help individuals recognize where their actions are hindering the organization from thriving and help them change their behavior. Together, individuals and the organizations in which they work have the power to take meaningful steps toward reimagining the workday.

CHAPTER 5

SETTING YOUR ORGANIZATION'S PACE

Let's do a quick check-in: at this point, I've
discussed why the way we're working isn't working.

I've introduced a framework for reimagining the workday in a way that
sticks: Work^Power.

Now, let's look closer at Organizational Pace and share our strategy for
setting a sustainable pace at your organization.

Part of setting a sustainable pace is regularly evaluating how fast you're
running (the pace at which you're working) and understanding which ways
of working are and aren't working for you and your organization.

According to Merriam-Webster, "pace" is defined as both a rate of
movement and a rate of *progress*. We want to always be making progress,
moving forward, improving, succeeding. But as with most things in life,
progress at work isn't linear, which is why it is so important to know where
we are starting and where we are going—so we don't lose stride along the way.

What does non-linear progress look like? We take leaps forward when we win a new client or finish a big project. Those are times for sprinting— and that can be fun! But we can't sustain the all-out sprint those seasons of work require. We have to be willing to put on the brakes, following periods of intensity with a slower pace, sometimes "coasting" for a while or stopping altogether by taking time off.

But the idea of pacing yourself at work goes far beyond a day off here and there or even a sabbatical. Everyone has their own optimal pace, and organizations themselves require different paces from their team and often different paces at different times.

A couple of years ago (okay, now that I think about it, over a decade ago), I had the opportunity to go to my cousin's wedding in the U.S. Virgin Islands. It was going to be a gorgeous five days, hanging out with family, enjoying good food (and rum!), and getting a fair amount of time alone to recharge.

Except... a client at work had a new opportunity for us to bid on, and conversations we'd been having for weeks turned into the chance for us to work on a "big proposal" the week before I was supposed to go. I was the one who had reeled in this particular opportunity, so I was the lead on the proposal. I had put my leave on the calendar, and everyone knew I was going out of town, so we (primarily I) rushed to get the proposal done. I worked hours and hours (on top of a regular workday) to get the proposal done. I worked on the plane on my way to the Virgin Islands, worked for my first day there, and spent the next two days recovering from a migraine. Happy vacation to me!

For what it's worth, I did still have a great time at my cousin's wedding and took a little truck to Trunk Bay on my last day to snorkel. But it certainly wasn't the five days of unplugging and rest I had both planned on and needed.

I put "big proposal" in quotes because these sudden, pressing needs at work are always big. And they always feel so critical. Now, as a business owner myself, I do see them all as important. But when these opportunities pop up, I think of that "demotivational poster" that shows a snowflake and says, "You're unique, just like everybody else." It always seems like these last-minute, all-out sprints at work are a one off—just this blip that happens to come when I had something planned. But have you ever stepped back to look at how common they might be? They're not that unique. And when aspects of our jobs are so critical that they consistently interrupt our vacation or weekend or evening, what that interruption really reveals is an inability to prioritize, inappropriately distributed work, insufficient training of team members, and poor boundaries.

I share this story because we've all been there. We block time off and spend weeks anticipating all the rest and fun we'll have. We need the break. But then our work gets in the way of true rest—and we end up right back where we started. This is the definition of working *off pace*.

So how, exactly, do you put pace in place at your organization? We use one main framework to guide and track our work on a client engagement: the *Pace Clock™*.

THE PACE CLOCK

Imagine the Pace Clock as a circle with four quadrants of "time": 12:00-3:00, 3:00-6:00, 6:00-9:00, and 9:00-12:00. Each quadrant corresponds to the stages of an engagement.

The Pace Clock (pictured below) is a way for people to visually see where they are on their journey to a sustainable pace, resulting in effectiveness. Every organization is different, with different pain points and different solutions, but the roadmap toward effectiveness is universal. Here is a glimpse into that journey.

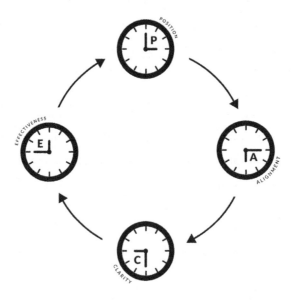

Position

For us to help a client, we need to understand where they are to understand their pain points and dig into why they've decided to rethink the way they work. There is often a breaking point for organizations that are struggling to work effectively. Maybe it's high turnover, poor performance, interpersonal conflict, or unsustainable levels of stress and burnout. You can't solve a problem you don't know (or aren't willing to admit) you have. While ideally, organizations would identify and address these pain points early on, it usually takes until they are wound so tightly into an organizational ball of chaos that they can't continue doing things the same old ways.

At MatchPace, we help organizations determine where they're starting on their journey to effectiveness—uncover their pain points and figure out what exactly about their workday is and isn't working—so we can help them create a roadmap. To do this, we use our signature **Pace Check**™ survey. The Pace Check is a quick, 20-question online survey to identify adaptive workforce performance and measure the pace of a team against what we've discovered are five Hallmarks of Organizational Effectiveness. These hallmarks are the distinctive traits that must be present and functional for an organization to attain success:

- **Vision & Strategy:** leadership-defined direction for the company, supported by leadership's words and actions, to measure other decisions against

- **Defined Accountability:** articulated lines of authority and responsibility within the organization and project teams, including what someone is and is not responsible for

- **Honesty & Trust:** willingness to be both upfront and vulnerable, committed to direct conversations and truthfulness

- **Healthy Work Experience:** the day-to-day experience of employees; enough freedom to encourage creativity and growth and enough boundaries to have direction

- **Structure for Sustained Growth:** the existence and maintenance of tools that support the vision; many tools can be automated but will require human use and "tending."

As you can see, the Hallmarks make their way around the Pace Clock, and that tells you what we work on in each quadrant of the clock. While the Hallmarks aren't divided perfectly into the four quadrants of the Pace Clock, we'll discuss each Hallmark in the first quadrant it appears in for simplicity. Keep in mind that just as in life and work, there is some fluidity to this process.

Any pain an organization may be feeling falls under one of those five Hallmarks of Effective Organizations, and the good news is that no organization is wound so tightly into a ball of chaos that they can't move toward an effective and sustainable pace. Before considering any change to the workday, it is critical to take a Pace Check and discover exactly how effectively—or ineffectively—your organization is operating.

If a team is burned out, why? Perhaps direction from managers or organizational leadership isn't clear, causing stress for team members who are always aiming for what feels like a moving target. Or maybe the total amount of work the team is expected to produce is just too much—unreasonable expectations are just as stressful as unclear expectations. Other common pain points include: a workday or workplace that maximizes distractions instead of focus (open office plans, anyone?), broken trust between team members and leadership, or employees feeling like they aren't safe to give constructive feedback to each other, managers, or leaders.

The answers to Pace Check questions reveal the team's perspective on their workplace, such as the clarity of the organization's vision, whether or not they know how their responsibilities connect to that vision, and what their day-to-day experience at work is like, including how they're feeling about balance and burnout.

The responses are anonymous and aggregated, and we're always looking for 100% participation from the team. If all voices aren't heard, we can't make appropriate steps that result in long-term changes for the organization that benefit everyone. Not to mention, leaving a group of people out of a conversation about what is and isn't working in a workplace is a key reason the same issues arise over and over again.

We also ask the organization's leadership to fill out the same survey, but *from the perspective of the team*—how leadership *thinks* the team feels. This allows us to track any disconnect between what the team knows, understands, and experiences and what leadership thinks the team knows, understands, and experiences.

It doesn't matter if the president of an organization thinks the vision is really clear. It matters if the president knows whether it's clear to the team or not. It doesn't matter if the president thinks the work-life balance is great; it matters if the president understands how the team experiences work-life balance.

The Pace Check is administered to both the organization's team and the leadership, and it informs our engagement to meet the individual needs of our clients. You have to know where you are, so we can help you solve the problems that are standing in the way of your effectiveness.

Alignment

"Bizspeak" is full of lots of fancy words that may or may not mean anything: "synergy," "incentivize," "paradigm shift." These terms aren't bad on their own, but we often roll our eyes when we hear them because of how many times they've served to make someone sound smart without actually meaning much.

Alignment has unfortunately become one of those "bizspeak" words that many may overlook, but alignment is actually critical to sustainable work. Once we've discovered your position—your pain points and what specific workplace policies are causing that pain, we know exactly where you are and why. Then, we help you articulate where you want to be, so we can figure out how to help get you there. Knowing where you are and where you want to be, then creating a route to get there, will bring your organization's workday and workplace into alignment with your mission, vision and values.

In the Alignment quadrant, we help you get the "bigger picture" things in place. These fall under the first three Hallmarks: Vision and Strategy, Defined Accountability, and Honesty and Trust.

If the Pace Check reveals that the organization's vision isn't clear, that's the best place for us to start—helping the organization articulate their mission and vision. I'll be frank that I've been surprised how often the vision isn't clear or leadership thinks they're going in one direction but actually change direction frequently. Or they think they're communicating the vision to their team, but the team isn't picking up what they're putting down. It's really hard for anything else to fall into place until the vision is clear.

We also work on Defined Accountability. Does the team understand what is required of each of them to help them reach that vision? Does the team understand what is inside and outside of their responsibilities? How can they count on others to be contributing to the vision?

The next part of alignment is Honesty and Trust. All of the Hallmarks are crucial, but this is perhaps the most important. It's hard to build trust and easy to break it, and it is foundational to each of the other Hallmarks. An organization with low trust experiences:

- Teammates with low morale leading to employee churn and high turnover
- Disengaged employees who fill a seat but don't care about your mission and aren't committed to organizational goals
- Distracted, unfocused, and uncreative employees
- High levels of conflict draining you and your organization of creativity and focus

In contrast, organizations with high levels of trust experience:

- Engaged employees committed to your mission and goals that stick around
- High levels of collaboration, creativity, efficiency, and focus
- A creative, agile team that reaches goals faster

We help organizations learn how to be both upfront and vulnerable, committed to direct conversations and truthfulness, enabling deeper effectiveness.

Clarity

So far, we've discussed the first two quadrants on our Pace Clock: We've helped an organization articulate their pain points, and unearthed what is causing that pain (through the Pace Check and the *Position* quadrant). We've determined or clarified their mission, vision, and values, clearly articulated roles and responsibilities, and made a concerted effort to build and embody trust within their organization (all within *Alignment*).

If those were the "bigger things," now we're able to work on the "smaller things." The things we work on in this stage aren't small in impact, but they can only come after you've made sure you have the first three Hallmarks in place. Do you remember earlier in the book when I said organizational change took a lot longer than I originally anticipated? At first I thought if I just demonstrated to everyone that there was so much waste in a given day and if they'd just stop allowing never-ending notifications to interrupt them, everyone would cry out, "My eyes have been opened!" and stop working ridiculously long, unsustainable, *ineffective* hours...

But I quickly realized that you can't shorten your hours if you don't know what it is you're supposed to be focusing on. You can't learn how to tell people no if you don't know what is actually yours to do and someone else's to do. If people don't trust one another, it doesn't work to shorten the workday because they'll always wonder if someone else can get their work done or assume the other person isn't pulling their weight.

So there's a lot of work to do *before* you can reimagine your workday. But now that everyone is on the same page about your vision, they know what their role is in supporting that vision, and deep trust has been established among the team, you can get to the part of our process where you actually change the way you work. You're ready to transform your workday from frantic, unnecessary overwork that is leaving people confused and burned out into a calmer, more focused, more engaged work environment that values people's attention and energy as well as their other priorities.

At this point, we're ready to address the *Clarity* of your day-to-day work—this is the third quadrant of the Pace Clock where we work on the remaining two Hallmarks: Healthy Work Experience and Structure for Sustained Growth (which, as you can see above, also happens in the final quadrant: *Effectiveness*).

It's not uncommon that the norms an organization is operating under (the unspoken and unwritten rules that dictate how an organization functions, which we'll discuss in-depth in the next chapter) are not in alignment with their values. By refining or redefining operating norms, an organization gives themselves the clarity they need to work well without getting wound into another organizational ball of chaos.

It might look like clarifying when they are supposed to be available and when they can turn their notifications off and focus on deep work. It can look as nuts-and-bolts as establishing protocols for how to run meetings, what information can be shared in an email versus what requires a person-to-person conversation, and how to track billable hours. When an organization lacks clarity in even the most mundane areas, breakdowns occur. And breakdowns are not only annoying, but they lead to stress and burnout and distract you from the deep work you need to do to accomplish your mission.

Once these first three quadrants are in place, we can get to one of my original goals when I started MatchPace: giving people back their time. It's at this stage that we develop a pilot for Core Hours (which I'll explain in detail in the next chapter).

Effectiveness

Finally, we've arrived at the last stop on the Pace Clock: Effectiveness. This is the ultimate goal for all organizations. When you work effectively, your team is working at a sustainable pace with clear norms in alignment with your organizational values. **You are getting the right things done at the right time with the right people in the right positions to produce the right outcomes that fuel your larger organizational mission and vision. That is what makes an organization effective.**

Organizational Effectiveness: Getting the right things done at the right time with the right people in the right positions to produce the right outcomes that fuel your larger organization mission and vision.

And, like most things in life, effectiveness isn't actually a destination but a journey unto itself. In this quadrant, we make sure that you build the scaffolding to sustain your organization (our last Hallmark, Structure for Sustained Growth) and solidify all the hard work you've done to create a sustainable pace.

This is where you get to enjoy all the pieces coming together: You and your team have greater clarity on your organizational vision. Trust among your team deepened and people know how to prioritize their most important work. Now, you can reimagine how you work and reap the benefits of investing your attention and energy in the right things while retaining attention and energy for other priorities, too.

An organization will always need to adapt to new clients and their changing needs, an ever-evolving workplace culture, turnover, leadership transition, technological advancements, and more. But you can use the Pace Clock and five Hallmarks to guide you towards effectiveness through any change.

THE PACE CLOCK IN ACTION

Do some of these things seem like a heavy lift? Or maybe you're thinking, *"Alignment with mission and values sounds good, but does it really make a difference in my day-to-day work? Can it help me be both more effective and actually satisfied at work?"*

Yes! We've figured out some key ways to track areas of organizational growth with data. Our real-world results show that yes, each dial matters, and they're key to setting an effective and sustainable organizational pace.

Before we share these real-world examples, we'd be remiss not to reemphasize that this isn't always a sequential or definite journey. Some organizations we work with already know their pain points or have a clearly articulated mission and values. Maybe they're starting their effectiveness journey at the Clarity stage. For others, the dial on the clock may swing back and forth due to leadership change at the organization, restructuring, an acquisition, or high turnover. It is possible for organizations, once working effectively, to lose clarity or slip out of alignment, surfacing new pain points with new challenges that need to be addressed.

We don't say this to discourage you—effectiveness is a worthwhile pursuit and worth the investment it takes to get there. Establish an organizational culture of sustainable effectiveness, and you'll remain nimble enough to quickly identify and address new pain points that allow you to stay in alignment. Give your team continued clarity, and operate in the effectiveness zone over the long haul at a sustainable pace.

At this point, let's walk through our journey with two real organizations we worked with using the Pace Check and Pace Clock.

Organization A

Organization A was a 15-person team whose Pace Check results revealed that their Position (the first dial on the Pace Clock) wasn't clear to the team. We were directly supporting the president of the organization, who, when shown the data from the Pace Check, believed us when we identified the team as far from clear on the values of the organization and how their roles and responsibilities supported those values and the larger mission.

Together, we set about clarifying the organization's Position. This involved:

- Codifying their organizational mission
- Helping the team articulate the values the organization aspires to
- Articulating roles and responsibilities, including clearly identifying a management structure (this clarified the weight of roles and the importance of team performance)

We then helped the organization move its major muscles into Alignment with the desired Position. We supported them as they :

- Established salary bands to increase transparency and equitable pay for all team members
- Developed a Code of Conduct to articulate how the team is expected to function from an ethical perspective
- Sought out training in diversity, equity, and inclusion (DEI) by teaming up with an external consultant

Once the major pieces were aligned, we could begin addressing "smaller tweaks": things that don't require large adjustments but take great strides toward a more sustainable working pace. They then began:

- Articulating a meeting structure to change how meetings are run, being more conscious of the content, intent, and responsibilities in meetings and working on changing organizational behavior

- Pursuing Core Hours, or articulated times for uninterrupted focus as well as collaboration

We continued to work on each of the above initiatives, along with regular coaching for leadership and managers and team retreats to help ensure these initiatives were successful and sustainable. This may sound like a lot of change all at once, so rest assured this process took time (and is still ongoing in the organization). But by getting their Vision and Strategy really clear (the first Hallmark of Effectiveness), the organization was able to support a sustainable effort for their team and remove the stressors that were leading to burnout.

Organization B

The second organization we worked with also had a 15-person team that felt like they were spinning their wheels. The team was getting some things done, but each effort was painful, and the team was burning out. We performed the Pace Check and just like Organization A, their Position wasn't clear. In fact, the focus of the organization wasn't really clear to the team or even to leadership. But the organization was a nonprofit, responsive to their most significant funder who was not providing a ton of leadership or direction, and had made it clear they weren't going to. This left the organization in a tight spot, characterized by confusion and frustration.

We tried, from several different angles, to help them advocate to their funder that they needed to spend time on clarifying their vision and mission to get a real sense of their Position (and they'd been asking for that clarity for years). But, the funder wasn't interested; they didn't see how helping the organization get their Position straight would help their bottom line and they liked that the organization was subject to their changing needs (even if it meant they weren't working effectively).

We have hopes that their funder will sooner rather than later agree to identify the right Position for the team, but in the meantime, we found a workaround: We helped the team create what they dubbed "interim values." They know these won't be their final actionable values, but they needed something to guide them, even while waiting (for years, maybe) for more clarity from their funder.

We stepped into the Pace Clock where they were, acknowledging that neither their current position nor where they want to go are clear, and we continue to work with them towards solutions. We have helped them clarify roles and responsibilities, as well as create some guiding principles that can live on, no matter the directions of their funder. We also instituted Core Hours, an instrumental element in their increased effectiveness. It is admittedly harder for them to sustain those Core Hours because they are at the mercy of changing priorities and projects. But they've established some norms around focus and collaboration that they try to sustain even in the face of unstable circumstances. They've set a sustainable pace they can return to any time their funder throws an obstacle in their path.

Organization B shows that even if you can't get every part and piece just right, you can still do things to measurably improve your team's lived experience and better accomplish your goal as you understand it.

Of course, I'd love to say both examples resulted in a magic "Voila!" moment and everyone lived (or at least worked!) happily ever after. But like any relationship, organizations require ongoing communication and adjustment.

Our experience with Organization B brings up a good point: **maintaining an effective pace hinges on a work culture that fully embraces the Pace Clock philosophy.**

It requires a culture—from the top bosses (or funders) to entry-level staff—that values focus and effectiveness. A culture willing to do the heavy lifting of changing patterns and habits (both organizational and individual) that don't help the team operate at their highest level. It requires boundaries that facilitate attention at work and allow team members to leave work (physically or virtually) and be fully present with other priorities. It rewards output—not just time clocked.

Not everyone will understand this. It requires a cultural shift for leadership (that they achieve through Work^3), funders, and even employees to catch on to the need to pursue a healthy, sustainable pace at work.

But our client results and MatchPace team experiences bear out. The right pace in your workplace will help you attract and retain top talent, maximize efficiency, and maintain a satisfied, productive workforce. And that kind of workforce will make you and your organization more efficient, effective, and successful for the long haul.

CHAPTER 6

THE MOST IMPORTANT QUESTION TO ANSWER BEFORE YOU RUN

L ET'S DIVE DEEPER INTO SOME OF THE ELEMENTS OF the Pace Clock and how they work in practice. One common sticking point for nearly every organization we work with is an organization's mission, vision, and values.

The idea of mission, vision, and values are likely familiar. We all know our organizations need clarity around what we do and why we do it, but we've found it's a lot harder for organizations to clearly articulate the foundation of their work.

When training for a race, you may find yourself falling short of your goals or giving up altogether if you don't first determine *why you're running.* Are you training to run alongside friends, like in my triathlon? Are you training to achieve a new personal record for distance run or fastest time? Are you running to maintain optimal health and fitness?

Without a "why," you'll find it easier to quit when the going gets tough. It's the same in life, too: Without understanding your personal values, your "why," you'll find it hard to push through seasons of stress or uncertainty. Your personal values are a tool you can use to determine if you are going in the right direction, if a particular decision is the right decision, or if you are headed in a direction that takes you further away from your goals and who you are.

While "values" can feel like one of those flimsy words that is hard to pin down and put into practice, you intrinsically know your values because when you're doing something that doesn't align with them, you feel off. When you're operating in alignment with them, you likely feel on! There's power in being able to name your values. If you've identified and articulated your core values, they serve as a "North Star," guiding you back when you've lost your way.

The same is true for organizations. Without *clearly articulated* values, it's difficult for a team—especially the larger it gets—to make the decisions they really want to make. And the sneaky thing about values is they're always there, whether you pay attention to them or not. If you don't take the time to outline your values as an organization, you may find both leadership and team members operating from values you don't want your organization to hold. Not having a shared and articulated "why" is a recipe for organizational disaster.

Not having clearly articulated values also prevents organizations from achieving all five Hallmarks of Organizational Effectiveness. From accountability to honesty and trust, a healthy work experience to sustained growth, murky values (or worse, values in name only and not in practice) prevent organizations from operating sustainably and effectively. So before we turn to the final concentric circle, our individual pace, we're going to spend some time unpacking how to set and sustain organizational values and norms.

CORE VALUES

Core values are the guiding principles of your life. As multifaceted individuals, we all have layers of values that guide who we are, what we do, and why we do them. Some values reside in the center of who we are and others are more peripheral and likely to shift as our roles and priorities change. But those peripheral values surround our core guiding values, and when we're not living out of those values (our core values), we lose our grounding.[17] You may not have ever named all your values, but when you're doing something that doesn't align with them, you know it.

The same is true as an organization. When team members hold different values or the values handed down by leadership are unclear or conflicting, everyone feels it. That's why there is power in being able to name your values—because then your team can evaluate a decision and determine which option is most in line with those clearly articulated values.

We often work with organizations to uncover, confirm, and articulate their core values. This is foundational to all of your decisions as a team— how you treat one another, how you engage with the people you serve, what it means to you to exist in the world, what you want to prioritize, and whether a particular decision, goal, or activity is in alignment with those values. Without clear values, you just can't work effectively. And without claiming a sustainable pace as a core value, you'll never achieve it.

ORGANIZATIONAL CORE VALUES EXERCISE

There are a number of exercises you can use to identify your organization's values. One that we enjoy doing with clients is this:

- Gather a small group that is representative of your organization (you should definitely include leadership, as they're the ones responsible for enacting these values, and also include teammates from other areas in the organization).

- Have each person write down three people they would like to work with at your organization—they could be famous people they admire or someone from their personal life.

- Have each person write down why they want those three people to work there—what traits they admire and would want to transport into their organization.

- Look for "threads" between those traits, and start making a list of similar traits, grouping them together.

- When you have identified common themes or groups of traits, choose one word that captures the essence of that trait, or what value those traits describe (we have a list of common values in our Core Values Exercise in the Appendix for inspiration).

- Discuss and select the most important three or four values from this exercise and order them by priority—which values you think are most important in your organization.

- Spend some time (during the meeting, after the meeting, or even a few months after) trying those values on for size—are those the defining characteristics you want to be true of your organization? Test out making decisions using them as your guiding principles.

PERSONAL CORE VALUES EXERCISE

While we haven't yet made it to the third circle (our pace as individuals), core values are incredibly important for each of us personally, too. Because our values undergird everything we do—even when we don't realize it—we encourage you to pause at this point in the book and take our *Core Values Exercise* with you as an individual in mind. It can be found in the Appendix or go to www.matchpace.net/resources, where you can complete it online within fifteen minutes.

VALUES VS. NORMS

We reference the concepts of values and norms throughout this book, as they intersect and determine your and your organization's ability to implement a sustainable working pace that achieves your organizational mission. Let's discuss the importance of norms and why values are impossible to put into practice without them.

If your **values** guide why you do what you do and inform the way you do it, **norms** are the often unspoken and unwritten rules about *how* you work. Values are the *why*, and norms are the *how*. Identifying your organizational norms and realigning them with your values is a critical step in the journey toward effectiveness. Norms should be expressions of your values, but often, we slip into patterns of norms that actually *contradict* our values.

Norms are rules that a group uses to define its appropriate and inappropriate attitudes and behaviors. They are both explicit and implicit; conscious and subconscious; stated and unstated; and sometimes even contradict each other. This is why norms can be so hard to pin down. Still, we operate based on norms in every area of our lives. Most importantly, our norms at work dictate how, where, and when we do our work, making them key to maximizing effectiveness and setting a sustainable pace.

Pause for a moment to think about the way your organization works in practice—not just how you say it works. For example, how does your team approach availability after work hours? Is it understood that evenings and weekends are yours? Or is it common for you to bring your laptop home on the weekends and regularly respond to clients or colleagues after hours? And if that is the case, is that expectation—or norm—to be available on weekends clearly stated? It's possible that managers are *saying* "Evenings and weekends are your own," but everybody knows they *really* expect you to be available to respond to clients and colleagues during evenings and weekends.

MatchPace helps clients uncover the "air quote" responses to the stated norm and clarify what it is really like to work at your organization (your current Position on the Pace Clock). Once you've unearthed that, you can decide if that's truly how you want to be working. Maybe you *do* want everyone to work nights and weekends. Okay—just say it out loud. It might impact the type of people who work for your organization, and it might impact the quality of work, but at least everyone will be on the same page. Or maybe you do want people to have their evenings and weekends to themselves, but it turns out they *think* you want them to be responsive all the time. Great! Now you can be clear about what you want, and you can help people adjust the way they are working to reflect that norm.

Below, we have a list showing examples of norms. There aren't "right" or "wrong" norms (as long as people are treated fairly and equitably), but norms *must* reflect the values of an organization, and be clear to all team members. This list of norms is far from exhaustive, but we hope it will get the juices flowing to help you identify all the norms your organization currently holds so you can evaluate them and adjust if necessary.

For example, for some companies, travel is non-negotiable. Employees can't really push back on travel if it's central to the work the organization does; if someone doesn't want to or is unable to travel, it's not the right organization for them. But organizations must be really clear with employees from the beginning about what expectations exist around travel. The last thing you want to do is advertise a job position with 20% travel, and then end up sending the person you hire out on the road 50% of the time. That pace will likely be unsustainable for them, they'll be ineffective in their work, and they'll burn out.

When we execute a norms survey with an organization, we work with the client to list the norms relevant to that organization and then ask people to respond whether or not they do those things and whether they think they *should or should not* do those things. That allows us to see what norms are currently in place and whether or not they are serving the organization and its team well.

Examples of Workplace Norms

- My role in meetings is generally clear.

- I have the freedom to make decisions in my role that are in the best interest of our clients.

- I bring my laptop home on evenings or weekends to work.

- I can tell when colleagues are doing focused work.

- I am able to use my judgement when considering client requests.

- I am expected to be fully engaged with a client project on a work trip.

- While traveling, I am expected to be engaged both with the client I am present with and with work going on in the home office.

- People on our team multitask during meetings, using computers or phones to work on other projects.

- I can adjust my travel schedule if personal demands require.

Whether you're in a position of leadership at your organization or not, encourage a conversation around norms. Ask yourself and your team to write down how you work, and then compare that against how you *want* to work and why.

CORE HOURS

Finally, our last stop on this journey before we move into the third concentric circle of Individual Pace is the concept of **Core Hours**. Core Hours, as you'll see, can be a transformational tool for restructuring how your organization works (those workplace norms) to help your entire team work at a sustainable pace.

Just like in triathlon training, if your daily pace doesn't allow you to sustain your work all the way through to the end of your goal (like a project deadline), you're going to underperform and end up worse off professionally and physically. And while there are certainly people who can run at a faster pace than me for a given length, our brains and our bodies, in general, are not built to speed through marathons of work every day—even if we think they should.

It's also important to match your pace with those around you, just like my two friends and I paced ourselves to complete our triathlon together. Keeping pace together required pushing ourselves harder in our not-so-strong areas and slowing down in others.

Just like training together, your organization needs to have established values, guidelines, and protocols about boundaries around focus and collaboration to produce a sustainable matched pace. Once those are in place, it's time to move on to the nuts and bolts of how to organize your workday as an entire organization. This isn't about efficiency tools or productivity hacks—it's about taking the lessons of this book on the why and how to set a sustainable working pace and putting it into practice.

Core Hours is a framework that we introduce to clients along their journey of reimagining their workday. Establishing norms around Core Hours is one of the most effective ways we see clients bring a reimagined workday to fruition. It will help you shape how and when a team collaborates so that everyone can do their best work, on pace, together.

Core Hours are agreed-upon blocks of time for how teams organize their days, weeks, and months. Core Hours dedicate time during the workday to engage in intentional collaboration and synergy while protecting other time for deep focus and creativity. They might even include a cadence of training days, all-team meetings, or times that everyone is simultaneously off from work to enable collective rest (so you don't come back from vacation to a flooded inbox and a huge to-do list).

Core Hours can be structured to fit every organization's mission, culture, and operations. They can include days or hours during which all staff are in the office or might only apply to times reserved for meetings and collaboration. But Core Hours only work *after* an organization has created an environment for them to work: a *visoin and strategy*, so everyone knows what they're supposed to focus on; *defined accountability*, so everyone knows what is theirs to do and what isn't; *honesty and trust*, so the team feels a sense of psychological safety, like they know what is going on and what is expected of them. You'll recall that these are three of the Five Hallmarks of Effectiveness, which we've already discussed at length. The Five Hallmarks continue to be the foundation for any "intervention" like Core Hours to actually work, instead of remaining some hack that doesn't last.

How an organization structures their Core Hours will be unique to them. An engineering firm may require lots of time set aside for deep focus while infusing blocks of time for collaboration. A communications firm may prioritize time for collaboration while also needing to ensure the team isn't constantly distracted from the focused, creative thinking required to deliver impact for their clients.

At MatchPace, we have created Core Hour frameworks that accommodate all sorts of needs, but there are common elements. These elements include: time set aside for meetings so that meetings don't slowly cannibalize a whole day of work; days and/or times all staff are together in person; and days or times specifically set aside for individualized focus.

If Core Hours sound too good to be true, don't just take our word for it. Organizations around the world are starting to rethink the way they structure their workday. They have discovered that making intentional changes to help their teams operate at a sustainable pace both increases productivity and boosts the employee experience.

For example, when Microsoft Japan closed its offices completely every Friday during August 2019, they found that "labor productivity increased by 39.9% compared with August 2018."[18] (It's important to note that full-time employees were still paid for those Fridays. When we talk about outcome-focused work, people should always be compensated for the outcome they produce, not the hours they spend to produce it.)

In the United States, many government agencies use alternative work schedules to give employees the flexibility they desire while maintaining a strong office culture.[19] The combination of autonomy with ownership of organizational culture can be a strong intrinsic motivator and result in greater productivity for staff.

Our experiences with clients tells the same story. MatchPace partnered with an organization to guide them in establishing a strong organizational structure to support their team during a time of rapid growth. We helped them craft a Core Hours framework that included:

- Redesigning weekly all-staff meetings, including the time, day, and structure, to focus meetings on the team's biggest priorities.

- Establishing a day completely without meetings for focus and deep work, and creating core meeting hours for the other days (hours that were designated for focus, hours that were designated for collaboration). This enabled teammates to know when they were expected to be available for in-person or virtual meetings, and clarified when they were free to work remotely.

- Establishing an "airplane day" policy that allowed staff to work with limited contact one day per day per month. (Remember that brief window when laptops were prolific but there wasn't WiFi on planes? You could get on a plane and knock out so much work! Thanks to not being able to go down internet wormholes or needing to respond to people's urgent needs, you had work done and emails lined up to go out as soon as you landed.) An airplane day allowed their staff to know they could put their heads down and just work. Some people used it as a day to work on important projects, while others used it to manage administrative tasks (nothing like getting that mandatory training off your plate, and how about a clean inbox, anyone?).

- A monthly "all-hands" day: a day that, barring personal needs, the team guarded from other commitments. Remote employees flew in, and travel for client needs was avoided. Sometimes they used that day for all-staff training, sometimes they used it for all-staff social events, and sometimes they just let it serve as an avenue for informal collaboration.

While habits are hard to change, this organization committed themselves to changing the way they worked. Leadership and staff were open to adjusting the culture and took great strides to improve processes that supported their team. And they made significant measurable progress: 78% of staff reported an increased ability to conduct focused work, 65% agreed there was an improvement in meeting effectiveness, and 89% of the staff felt committed to sustaining the changes they had made—which, when we checked in with the organization three years after our work with them, they were still practicing. Now that's what we call real, lasting change!

Need some more inspiration for setting Core Hours? At MatchPace, we personally use Monday as a "reset" for the week and a time to dedicate the day to deep work and focus (what we call "No Meeting Monday"). We suggest dedicating the day to your most important task for the week and setting aside one to two hour-long blocks for email and administrative work. This focuses the majority of the day for deep work.

Of course, client needs do sometimes arise on Mondays, but we do our best to establish early on with clients that we prioritize meetings mid-week, and a simple "I'm not available Monday. Could we look at Tuesday?" usually works.

Tuesdays through Thursdays, we ask team members (particularly consultants) to be available for collaboration and to prioritize client meetings and work. We hold a team call every other Tuesday morning, which is a team non-negotiable.

Just as you might block off a day of the week for deep work and focus, it is equally important to set aside time *daily* for deep work, especially if you spend the bulk of your time in collaboration or client services. On days dominated by meetings, we still block off 60-90 minutes of time for deep work so that we aren't simply running from one thing to the next and can actually get some work done. We commit to not scheduling client meetings or other collaboration during those blocks of time, even if the time of day we block off for deep work shifts, depending on our schedule each week.

Finally, we use Fridays for administrative work and to tie up any loose ends from the week. This is a great time to catch up on non-urgent emails as well as wrap up any projects before the weekend. We also spend some time looking ahead to determine our *priority* (yes, just one!) for the next week, so we can dedicate the beginning of our Monday to our most important task.

It must be said that these are the Core Hours that work for us as an organization—we're a client services company with people expecting reasonably timely responses. While you could take elements of them, your unique organization will require its own unique set of Core Hours to meet the needs of your team and clients. But we hope painting a picture of the norms we use to foster focus and creativity and make the best use of our time helps you start to imagine a set of Core Hours that can help your organization set a sustainable working pace.

CHAPTER 7

MAKING HYBRID WORK

———

WHEN WE STARTED MATCHPACE, WORKING FROM home was usually an arrangement reserved for special circumstances or the occasional organization (usually a startup)–not a common workplace norm. Then, just as we started writing this book, the Coronavirus (COVID-19) pandemic hit.

COVID-19 upended the way an entire generation works—knowledge workers, in particular. Organizations across industries and geographies had to figure out how to work remotely almost overnight, and over one year later, we emerged into a new world of work.

Now, organizations are regrouping and asking themselves, "How should we work now?" Jobs we always thought would be impossible to do remotely are now being done regardless of location. Some people chose to use the flexibility of remote work to relocate closer to family or to cities with a lower cost of living. Organizational leaders who never would have approved remote or flexible work prior to the pandemic now feel like they don't have much of a choice if they want to retain their best employees.

Before we move on to the next concentric circle of Individual Pace, we want to take a brief detour and talk about the unique challenges and opportunities that come with a hybrid work environment and how to use the power of pace to ensure both in-person and remote team members can work effectively together.

As organizations began to think about returning to work, the CEO of Spotify boldly claimed, "The 9-to-5 workday is dead," and decided to let Spotify employees work from anywhere. Meanwhile, Google initially said they expected almost everyone back in the office, later relaxing requirements to three days a week when they experienced push back. But Google was still clear that they wanted their workforce within commuting distance of an office and to be in the office regularly. (And, of course, they've made further adjustments since then, reflecting the hard work of figuring these things out.) So who is right? What is the right way to work post-pandemic—or any time, for that matter?

The answer: there isn't one *right* way to work. There never has been, and there certainly isn't now. Instead, each organization must assess the unique needs of their employees and clients and determine the right way for *them* to work.

While some organizations, because of those unique needs, will bring all employees back to the office full time, others are choosing to go fully remote, with a distributed workforce and no central office. Still others—likely most organizations—will choose to allow their employees flexibility in location and hours, and they will find themselves somewhere on a "hybrid scale," especially if companies want to hold on to valued employees who might seek a more remote-friendly workplace. This means some employees within the same organization will work full time in the office, others will work exclusively from remote locations, and others will strike a balance between days in the office and days at home.

While a hybrid work environment creates new opportunities for organizations to attract and retain top talent and offer their teams some much-needed flexibility and balance, organizations face a new set of challenges setting a sustainable pace for teams across multiple locations, time zones, and working hours. However, a thoughtful approach to hybrid work might be the solution we've all been searching for: an opportunity to create work-life balance and enhance equity in the workplace that wasn't possible with the way we were working pre-pandemic.

OUTCOME-FOCUSED WORK IN A HYBRID ENVIRONMENT

Outcome-focused work has never been more necessary. Regardless of how an organization chooses to position its team geographically and physically, one thing is true: Organizations that want to succeed in this new world need to shift to outcome-focused work.

A shift away from managing *time* toward managing *outcomes* is critical for remote workers who don't have the built-in structure of an office setting to keep them on task. Working from home blurs the line between the professional and the personal as the office comes home. Many remote workers have fallen prey to the pressure of constant availability from the moment their eyes open until their head hits the pillow at night. An at-home setting that should be giving them more autonomy is actually just forcing them to work longer.

That's where outcome-focused work and Core Hours come in. They take the pressure off of wondering when to be available, fighting to fit a set number of hours of work into a day filled with constant interruption and competing priorities. Instead, team members can manage their own time, knowing when they are expected to be available for collaboration, when they can focus, and exactly what they need to accomplish in a given day.

Outcome-focused work also shifts the burden off of managers to make their team "look busy" all day long. Managers can trade late-night emails and pointless standing meetings for workday structures that reward effectiveness, giving team members the autonomy they crave whether they're in the office or working at home.

Prior to COVID-19, we used to ask the question, "How would your workweek look if your goal wasn't to clock a certain number of hours but to achieve specific outcomes and then go home and unplug?" With many employees choosing to work from home, managing outcomes versus time is even more important to prevent burnout because unplugging looks different when your laptop is always arms' length away.

IN-PERSON FIRST OR REMOTE-FIRST?

Managing the pace of hybrid teams can feel daunting. How can organizational leaders balance the diverse range of workforce needs, client needs, resource distribution, communication, collaboration, team morale, performance reviews, opportunities for advancement, and more when their teams are no longer together all day, every day?

These are significant challenges for organizations, but they are also significant opportunities to reimagine the future of work. When figuring out how your organization will work in a hybrid environment, we've found that choosing to manage either as a "Remote First" organization or an "In-Person First" organization offers the clarity leadership and employees need to work together successfully. This eliminates the potential for confusion and conflict between employees working from different locations and helps organizations set clear norms around how to work together.

Organizations who want to work better—with more focus, more collaboration, less burnout, and greater equity—than they were pre-pandemic will need to ask themselves a series of questions through the lens of whether they are going to manage their teams as Remote First or In-Person First. As you'll see below, the first question to ask yourself when setting up a hybrid work environment is "what type of work requires what type of environment?" Instead of thinking about anyone's personal preferences (which are likely competing), think first of your mission, the responsibilities of each person in your organization, what kind of work they do, and what kind of environment best supports that work.

One way to consider the distinction is to think about who will make the bulk of the accommodations when decisions are made: in-person employees or remote employees? While "burden of accommodation" sounds kind of weighty and negative, the truth is that some people will have to make more accommodations than others in a hybrid environment, even in mutually beneficial relationships. Who will the burden of accommodation fall on? When you've named them and been honest about those accommodations across your organization, you can keep an eye on them and make sure they don't get too burdensome.

Take the simple example of scheduling meetings. Organizations who have been meeting exclusively virtually throughout the pandemic now have to decide how to execute meetings when some employees are in the office and others are remote, sometimes in different time zones. In a Remote First organization, the balance tips toward remote employees and in-person employees must make accommodations for their remote colleagues. This looks like scheduling all meetings virtually between standard working hours across the time zones employees are located in—for example, not until 11 a.m. Eastern Time so West Coast colleagues can attend the meeting during normal business hours.

On the flip side, in an In-Person First organization, the remote employees will have to make the bulk of the accommodations. In this case, looking at the same example, employees in an East Coast office know they have the go-ahead to schedule meetings at 9 a.m. Eastern, and those in the Pacific time zone will have to flex their work hours to make a 6 a.m. Pacific meeting.

Neither of these norms are wrong–but one might be wrong for *your* organization. That's why it's critical for organizational leaders to assess what works best for their team and clients, and then *clearly communicate* their expectations as a Remote First or In-Person First organization.

That's a key point we want to spend some time on: **Leadership should clearly communicate expectations**. In a May 2021 article in the Harvard Business Review, Nicholas Bloom, an Economics Professor from Stanford University, shared that some employers have the perspective of "treating their employees like adults. They get to decide when and where they work, as long as they get their jobs done."

But he cautioned organizations to consider the equity issues inherent in that kind of approach. There is a risk of creating an office "in-group" and a home "out-group" (even when trying hard not to). And the "choose your own adventure" approach can be a threat to diversity. Employees who work from home are at a significant disadvantage for opportunities and promotion. And when you examine who typically chooses to work from home (parents, predominantly women) and who has the ability to come into the office every day (a lot of single young men), you risk jeopardizing the diversity of your team which, he says, puts you at risk for possible discrimination.[20]

Deciding whether your organization will operate as In-Person First or Remote First should not become about control—by either employers or employees. The conversation must go beyond thoughts like "I never want to go back to the office" or "If people aren't in the office, it means they don't want to hustle." This decision-making framework is about accomplishing your mission and doing so in the most equitable way possible. It's about taking each other's perspectives and needs into consideration, accommodating one another.

The bright side? The pandemic has given us an opportunity to reconsider our existence in so many ways. We get to draw a new map for ourselves organizationally, professionally, and personally.

Below is the full Hybrid Scale framework for making decisions as an In-Person First or Remote First organization. This is the set of questions we use to walk organizations through the transition to hybrid work, and we want you to have access to it so you have the greatest chance of success of implementing a hybrid workscape that is equitable, effective, and sustainable.

IN-PERSON FIRST   # REMOTE FIRST

ACTIVITY-BASED WORK

IN-PERSON FIRST	REMOTE FIRST
• Which kinds of work require which type of environment?	• Which kinds of work require which type of environment?

WORKSPACE

IN-PERSON FIRST	REMOTE FIRST
• How will the costs of remote workers' needs be handled? (e.g., software, office space, office supplies, etc. – do they pay, organization pays, or a mix?	• How much and what kind of office space is needed, if any, and where (including how many locations)?

EMPLOYEE STATUS

IN-PERSON FIRST	REMOTE FIRST
• What are the considerations for people wanting to change from In-Person to Remote status or vice versa over time? • What are the "rules of engagement" for "occasional" remote work (e.g., case-by-case, or by employee type/role, or ...)? • How will we adapt to the tax realities of having employees in different states and municipalities?	• What are the considerations for people wanting to change from Remote status to In-Person or vice versa over time? • What are the "rules of engagement" for "occasional" in-person work (e.g., when employees in the same geographic area choose to hold in-person meetings)? • How will we adapt to the tax realities of having employees in different states and municipalities?

HOUSEHOLD RESPONSIBILITIES

IN-PERSON FIRST	REMOTE FIRST
• What flexibility do in-office employees have to respond to family needs?	• How are remote employees expected to handle the day-to-day needs of children or partners at home? • What expectations do those working from home need to consider if/when family needs arise?

IN-PERSON FIRST   REMOTE FIRST

EQUITY

- How do we support remote employees who don't have access to passive information flow?
- How do we mitigate the concerns among in-person employees that remote employees have more flexibility or other lifestyle advantages than they do?
- How do we ensure remote employees have equitable access to opportunities (participation, advancement, etc.) that in-person employees have access to?
- How do we ensure equitability in managing and evaluating employee outputs/outcomes?

- How do we accommodate employees who do not have the resources to work remotely (e.g., office space in their homes, high-speed WiFi)?
- How do we ensure equitability in managing and evaluating employee outputs/outcomes?
- How will we neutralize unconscious bias based on seeing into someone's home?

EMPLOYEE ENGAGEMENT AND MORALE

- How do we make remote employees feel included and part of the team and culture? How will we build team morale in a dispersed environment?
- What benefits will the organization provide with "hybrid realities" in mind, including mental health support for team members (in-person vs. remote) who might feel more isolated, have special needs, etc.?
- What are the strategies/tactics we will use to minimize differences in perceived value from those working in-person vs. remotely?

- How do we build trust, confidence, and camaraderie among employees who are rarely, if ever, in person together? (Including new hire training, team retreats, etc.)
- What benefits will the organization provide with "hybrid realities" in mind, including mental health support for team members (in-person vs. remote) who might feel more isolated, have special needs, etc.?
- What are the strategies/tactics we will use to minimize differences in perceived value from those working in-person vs. remotely?

IN-PERSON FIRST   REMOTE FIRST

COMMUNICATIONS

IN-PERSON FIRST	REMOTE FIRST
• How do we establish Core Hours that enable true collaboration while not expecting everyone to be available all the time? How do we ensure communication to and from remote employees are timely, accurate, and relevant without requiring being constantly "on"?	• How do we establish Core Hours that enable true collaboration while not expecting everyone to be available all the time? How do we ensure communication, in general, is timely, accurate, and relevant when conducted largely virtually?

WORK HOURS NORMS

IN-PERSON FIRST	REMOTE FIRST
• How do we set working hours fairly and reasonably to be responsive to our clients, acknowledge the headquarter office timezone, and so remote employees are not disadvantaged beyond reasonableness? • How do we establish Core Hours that foster collaboration with remote colleagues as well as allowing time for employees of either status to focus?	• How do we set working hours so work organization-wide is optimized for efficiency and flow if employees and/or clients are in different time zones? • How do we establish Core Hours that enable true collaboration while not expecting everyone to be available all the time?

RESPONSIBILITIES

IN-PERSON FIRST	REMOTE FIRST
• What new responsibilities emerge related to coordinating the activities of hybrid teams? Will this require more responsibility for management, additional team members, or both? • How might such new responsibilities be assigned/ entrusted, and/or rewarded differently based on in-person or remote status?	• What new responsibilities emerge related to coordinating the activities of hybrid teams? Will this require more responsibility for management, additional team members, or both? • How might such new responsibilities be assigned/ entrusted, and/or rewarded differently based on in-person or remote status?

IN-PERSON FIRST   REMOTE FIRST

ROLE ASSIGNMENTS

- What roles, if any, can only ever be done by in-person employees?
- What are the implications for fairness in advancement potential and other HR dimensions?
- Will in-person employees be allowed to elect roles on an individual basis, based on location status, or are there other variables?

- What roles, if any, may be best suited to only ever be done by remote employees?
- What are the implications for fairness in advancement potential and other HR dimensions?
- Will remote employees be allowed to elect roles on an individual basis, based on location status, or are there other variables?

ACCOUNTABILITY

- How do we provide remote employees regular access to what in-person employees are doing?
- How do we ensure managers are adequately trained to manage in-person and remote teams?

- How do we monitor and measure what remote employees are doing in ways that don't place an unreasonable "burden of proof" on them?
- How do we ensure managers are adequately trained to manage remote teams?

CLIENT INTERACTION

- How do we handle client assignments? (e.g., are clients based all in one geographic location or time zone, or are both employees and clients dispersed across geography?)

- How do we handle client assignments? (e.g., are clients based all in one geographic location or time zone, or are both employees and clients dispersed across geography?)

HIRING

- Will hiring decisions be based mainly on location, and how will skills/fit of remote employees be considered fairly?

- How will cost differentials of people in different locations be factored in fairly? (Including compensation, benefits, client billing, etc.?)

You can use these questions to figure out whether you're an In-Person First organization or a Remote First organization, and you can use them to ensure you're addressing any of the potential challenges that come with either orientation.

Now, let's get back to learning how we can set a sustainable working pace for ourselves and our organizations today while remaining agile in the face of the change we know will inevitably face us as we adapt to a new way of working. Fortunately, the principles of pace apply regardless of whether we work in an office or at home.

Let's turn to the innermost concentric circle: our pace as individuals. Of course, organizations are made up of different people with different individual paces, which, when combined, create both challenges and opportunities for setting a sustainable working pace together. We can't wait to introduce you to a tool that has transformed our own work experiences, individually and together.

CHAPTER 8

THE CHRONOPACE™

———

NOW IT'S TIME TO LOOK AT OPTIMIZING OUR PACE AS an individual. You may have noticed one common challenge to setting a sustainable organizational pace: What happens when different people operate best at different paces? Some people are naturally better at sprinting while others excel in sustained effort over time. You may not even know the right pace to set for yourself, let alone your organization as a whole. And your team is likely full of both early birds and night owls, as well as those who work best with long blocks of sustained focus and those who thrive in collaborative environments.

That's where the ChronoPace™ comes in. *"And what,"* you might be thinking, *"...is a ChronoPace?"* We're glad you asked!

The human body operates on a 24-hour internal clock. You sleep, wake up, and experience a rhythm of energy peaks and valleys over the course of the day. And while no two people operate on the exact same internal clock, there are four **chronotypes** or categories that most individuals fall into.

Chronotypes are the emotional and behavioral patterns associated with a person's internal clock. But these aren't set in stone—research indicates that your chronotype can change over the various seasons of your life. While you may have been able to focus late into the evening at one time in your life (like those all-nighters you pulled in college), new responsibilities and life circumstances may now require an adjusted sleep-wake pattern, shifting your peak focus period.

In addition to your chronotype, your body also cycles through 90-120-minute activity-rest periods called *ultradian cycles*. Taken together, your chronotype and ultradian cycles help identify the best times of day to perform different tasks based on your optimal mood, energy, and focus.

UNDERSTANDING THE CHRONOPACE

ChronoPace is the way MatchPace frames chronotypes and ultradian cycles, identifying the natural rhythms of your body to help you work better.[21] Substantial research has been conducted on the importance of pacing for peak physical performance[22] and optimal health.[23] These theories confirm that determining your peak and off-peak productivity periods will help you identify your most effective self and sustain your pace in your professional and personal lives. The more that you understand your natural rhythms, the better equipped you are to plan ahead and schedule activities accordingly.

Additionally, identifying different work styles across members of an organization can help determine the best way to collaborate and synthesize strengths among teams. We'll share some tips for helping bring a team with diverse ChronoPaces into alignment, but first, it's important to understand the implications that different rhythms have for the workday.

Just as there are four main chronotypes, there are four ChronoPaces with different peak performance times during the day:

- **Early Morning Pacer:** Peak performance times for these individuals are 5 a.m. - 10 a.m.

- **Mid-Morning Pacer:** Peak performance times for these individuals are 7 a.m. - 12 p.m.

- **Afternoon Pacer:** Peak performance times for these individuals are 10 a.m. - 3 p.m.

- **Evening Pacer:** Peak performance times for these individuals are 5 p.m. - 1 a.m.

It is important to structure your day to ensure you are able to give your personal and professional best to the things most important to you. Structuring your workday for maximum productivity requires planning how you'll spend your time and attention and using your peak performance times to your advantage.

Save your more routine tasks—those requiring less complex problem-solving or attention to detail—for your non-peak performance times. Good ways to utilize your non-peak hours would be scheduling or participating in routine meetings, checking email, organizing your schedule, and checking in with coworkers, which are all important parts of producing good work and maintaining strong professional relationships.

Utilize breaks that match the work you're doing. If you're doing deep focused work, take a solitary break and allow your mind to wander. If you're in the middle of collaboration, take a social break and chat with the colleagues you're working with. Choose activities that are actually restful—a 10-minute walk, five deep breaths, being still for 60 seconds—and avoid things that look like rest but really aren't (like checking email or social media).

Understanding your own pace has another advantage: It helps you understand that other people have different paces. Just like learning about someone's Myers Briggs Type Indicator (MBTI) or their Enneagram number teaches you to interact with them more effectively, the same is true in learning about someone's ChronoPace. When you understand their working pace, you can leverage it to your advantage (just like my team knows to send requests to me in the early morning if they want my best attention).

I happen to be an Early Morning Pacer. Although many Early Morning Pacers will act like there is, there is nothing more righteous about early birds than any other types. I think that comes from Early Morning Pacers being able to get their deep work done before the chaos of the day sets in, which comes with the perception that they're "ahead" of everyone else. Our culture also tends to praise early birds, with conventional wisdom telling us that getting up earlier makes us more productive. But if you're an Evening Pacer, you'll struggle to do your best work early in the morning when your ChronoPace tells you that you should be resting. Evening Pacers naturally do their deep work at the end of the day, but that doesn't mean they're falling behind. Ultimately, you want to get your work done in the most effective, focused way possible for you and your organization—that's what matters!

As an Early Morning Pacer, I know that my best days actually start the night before—putting my phone away early, reading, and getting a peaceful transition into sleep so that I can wake up refreshed. My ideal day looks like this: wake up at 5am, do some spiritual grounding/meditation, get an hour or two of deep work in, exercise, greet my family and help them start their days, have some late-morning/early-afternoon meetings and… that's about all I'm good for. A 3 p.m. or 4 p.m. meeting generally does not bode well for me with my ChronoPace. And remember how protective parents of teenagers might say something like, "Nothing good happens after midnight"? For me, nothing good really happens after 8 p.m. I'm tired, my brain is fried, and when I try to work, unless it's on a very specific deliverable with an imminent due date, I generally wander around the internet not actually getting anything done. I end up going to bed late, resulting in a rough start the next day. (And think of that from a "billable hours" perspective - theoretically if I needed to charge hours, I could charge for that 8-10pm that I spent trying to work. I didn't produce anything of value for a client, but I "put in hours.")

Obviously, not every day is centered around my work, and not all workdays are "ideal" workdays. But now that I know how I best function, I can create opportunities to work in a way that reflects my unique pace–professionally and personally. I'm able to help my teammates understand how I work best, and I can understand them and try to work with their Chronotypes. (Shout out to a former colleague who did her best work at 2 a.m.! We couldn't move client meetings to 11 p.m., but I tried hard to not expect her to reply to emails first thing in the morning or attend early morning meetings!)

As you understand your own ChronoPace, and the ChronoPaces of your team, you are one step closer to leveraging those different paces and establishing a collective pace that works for all of you. When you know each other's ChronoPaces, you can use that information to influence your Core Hours, and your everyday interactions.

CHRONOPACE EXERCISE

To take the five-minute ChronoPace Quiz and discover your own ChronoPace, go to www.matchpace.net/resources. Write down your quiz results below, for future reference.

My ChronoPace™ type is _____ .

In the Appendix, you will find four sample ChronoPace schedules, one for each of the four ChronoPaces: Early Morning, Mid-Morning,

Afternoon, and Evening Pacers. Based on your results from the ChronoPace quiz, you may find structuring your day around these sample schedules helpful, especially if your current schedule does not optimize your peak and non-peak hours. It's important to note that these are schedules intended to optimize a workday; if work is not your highest priority (such as if you are a stay-at-home parent), you can adapt the schedule to ensure your peak and non-peak hours fit your needs.

We can't always have total control over our days, but I've found that when I'm off my ChronoPace, it helps to simply be aware that I'm doing an activity at a suboptimal time. And making sure I give myself a few windows each week to really "run" during my peak times fuels me when I have to keep on moving, even during a low-energy time of day. As you begin to shift your schedule to optimize peak and non-peak hours based on your ChronoPace, take careful note of your energy and focus levels and make adjustments as necessary. While the majority of us fall within one ChronoPace type, our ultradian rhythms are unique, and you may find shifting the schedule slightly helps you take full advantage of your peak and non-peak hours.

The ChronoPace tool is, bby far, a favorite of our readers and clients. There's a fascinating science to timing. If you'd like to learn even more, Daniel Pink's book *When* is a gold mine for multidisciplinary research into the timing of, well, everything. And when it comes to when we work, Pink affirms something we all can feel but don't always accommodate: 2:55pm is scientifically the worst minute of the day (did you notice how no one really has their peak time in the mid-afternoon?). One small step toward pacing yourself is to remember to not schedule any important work during that window!

THE CHRONOPACE FOR TEAMS

The ChronoPace is intended to help individuals determine their optimal working pace, but what happens when you have people with different ChronoPaces on your team?

The first step is to understand what types of Pacers you have on your team, among leadership, and in your larger organization. Some of our clients have had fun sharing their results with each other and watching the light bulbs go off when they realize that someone isn't intentionally coming in "late" every day but instead has their most productive time from 11 p.m. - 1 a.m.

Once you've established the different ChronoPaces on your team, one approach is to try to set up a schedule that accommodates the majority of them. If your team is composed of a lot of Early Morning Pacers, don't schedule meetings before 11 a.m., so they can use the morning hours for deep focus. Schedule meetings in the late morning and early afternoon, and expect everyone to wrap up their work around 3 p.m.

If you work with a group of Evening Pacers, then you *still* don't have meetings before 11 a.m. You may not even start your workday until mid-morning. You'll also have reasonable expectations around when people will get their most focused, impactful work done—likely toward the end of the workday or even after traditional work hours. Consider scheduling meetings at the designated start of your team's workday (not to be confused with 9 a.m.) and encourage deep work later in the day.

The key is to not expect everyone to work all the time. That's what happens a lot in organizations with a variety of ChronoPaces: The CEO is a night owl and sends emails at 11 p.m., so people think they have to stay up late to be responsive. This bodes poorly for Early Morning and Mid-Morning Pacers, who suffer when they stay up too late and aren't able to maximize their early productive hours. Set norms and Core Hours that empower people to do their best work at the optimal time, and be flexible with those with different ChronoPaces.

Understanding the ChronoPace, instituting Core Hours, and being clear about norms (like teaching that CEO to use the "send later" button available in their email client) will go a long way towards a more harmonious, sustainable pace for everyone in your organization and help you maximize your effectiveness.

CHAPTER 9

PUTTING PACE IN PLACE

A T MatchPace, the foundation of our work with clients is teaching them the importance of pace and how to optimize it at work, both as an individual and as an organization. We know the idea of pace can feel theoretical and even aspirational. We'd all love to be working at our optimal ChronoPace and align that pace with our organization, but is it really possible in practice?

The reality is, while I'm the founder of MatchPace, I'm also a client. I started MatchPace because I care *so* much about good work but not so much that I wanted to have it consume my entire life. I love to do good work, but I have often felt like my days were a mishmash of meetings that didn't quite have a point or repetitive work that had outlived its usefulness.

In this chapter, I want to share how I apply MatchPace principles in my personal and organizational life. It should go without saying by now that Individual Pace and Organizational Pace are two sides of the same coin. My aim is to shed light on both by sharing how I pursue a sustainable pace.

NON-NEGOTIABLES

By now, we've established the important role that pace plays in keeping our work sustainable. But the solutions we use to solve the problem of a frantic pace will be unique because we each have our own unique pace set by our circumstances, season of life, role, and type of work.

So, what solutions have I found to keep a sustainable pace in my own personal and working life?

Remember those Core Hours we've discussed? My non-negotiables are in many ways a reflection of this and other organizational norms. They also reflect the values I have identified for myself and my ChronoPace type.

First, as I mentioned previously, I created "No Meeting Mondays," and I guard my time and attention that day like my life depends on it (some weeks, it feels like it does!). It's taken time and practice, but I help my team, clients, and even family understand that generally my attention is not available on Monday mornings from 6 a.m. to noon (my husband handles our children and any related needs). That gives me six uninterrupted hours of deep work, so I can focus on the most important tasks for that week. On my best Mondays, that means I don't even open my email before noon! This ensures *I* set the agenda for the morning (and even week) instead of reacting to the needs of others and letting *them* set my agenda. I love those Mondays!

It has taken practice to bring intentional windows of deep work into my week, but there is no more powerful tool to help me accomplish my priorities and prevent burnout. Most people are most effective and focused when they first wake up, but a lot of us have a chaotic mish-mash greeting us in the morning. Try giving yourself even two hours one or two days a week right when you wake up, and discover how giving yourself the freedom to focus transforms your workweek. (I personally know how hard that is if you have family responsibilities—like I said, different solutions will work in different seasons of life.)

If it is within your power to set aside intentional windows of deep work, you'll find that giving yourself that time can actually make you feel better! Are you familiar with the concept of "flow" coined by Mihály Csíkszentmihályi? Flow is your mental state when you are completely immersed in one activity or event. Research shows that people who experience flow on a regular basis have lower levels of depression and anxiety. And the opposite is true: Lack of flow can lead to depression and anxiety (like we talked about in the section on burnout).

I encourage you to see if you can make it happen: try to find two or three hours where you have enough time to actually get into a groove, close off all interruptions and see if you can get lost in an activity, whether "work" work or something else you find engaging. The time you spend in flow will not be "lost" but actually found time when you emerge renewed and reengaged.

Beyond "No Meeting Mondays," I hold other blocks of time each week for non-negotiables, like "Admin Catch-up" on Fridays—all that stuff that needs to be done but doesn't feel critical in the moment and is the oil that keeps the gears turning.

On the personal side, Sunday movie night with my family is non-negotiable. Instead of doing dishes or folding laundry (as parents are so often doing while "spending time together"), I push all the household chores to the side so that I can be truly present with my husband and kids. I won't always be able to spend an evening with a kid—or three—sitting on my lap, singing along to a movie. They will soon have sports, friends, and other commitments, and right now, this is non-negotiable for me.

Remember, while we all should build these non-negotiables into our routine, they will change over time.

Before I had kids, I worked out four to five days each week and often went on 10-mile runs (not fast, mind you!). Exercise is still non-negotiable for me, but it looks like a weekly pilates class, a weekly strength training class, and walking to client meetings instead of more gym time or long runs. Right now, I'm focused on building my family and business, so sustaining a basic level of activity is enough for me in this season. In a few years, that will change.

A pro tip is to actually overbook your week with non-negotiable blocks because life will inevitably get in the way. I had a coaching client who was a tenure-track college professor and tried to block off the writing time they needed to achieve their goals. They were disappointed that their writing time was often eaten up by other things (short-notice faculty meetings, emergent student needs, childcare hiccups). Through our conversations, they came to realize that if they thought they needed a minimum of three writing sessions each week, they should actually block off time for five. That way, if two were interrupted, they could still hit their target. Did it mean they could do "less" overall, because they didn't have room in their schedule? Yes, but it actually resulted in them getting *more* done - more important work! While not resenting inevitable interruptions.

Personally, I use what I call the "85% Non-Negotiable" rule: This means I shouldn't be flexing my non-negotiables more than 15% of the time. For example, as mentioned, I generally try to keep Mondays free of meetings. But sometimes, a client schedules their retreat on a Monday and Tuesday. So I flex, but keep an eye on my calendar—have I "flexed" more than one or two Mondays in a six-week period? If so, something is out of alignment.

Keep an eye on your non-negotiables. Have you "flexed" (or missed) more than 15% of the time? If so, check in and see what you need to do to get back on track.

If you struggle to stick with your non-negotiables, it might help to take a "time inventory" by tracking exactly how you spend your time each week—be as specific as you can. It may feel cumbersome, but very few of us have a true picture of where our finite time goes.

One common distraction that sucks up hours of our week is our smartphones (endless scrolling, anyone?). I don't keep my phone in my bedroom unless my husband is traveling, and on my best days, I'm able to resist the urge to look at my phone first thing in the morning, giving me time with my thoughts before being bombarded by someone else's. This is a great practice to help you hone your ability to focus.

BOUNDARIES

If establishing non-negotiables and putting your optimal pace in place are the exercises necessary to build a strong, sustainable workday, then boundaries are the muscles you need to stretch and strengthen to maintain that pace.

Boundaries are one of those "buzzwords" that get tossed around a lot in advice columns, but they're surprisingly hard to set and, more importantly, enforce. What good is a boundary if you're always crossing it? We have traffic lanes for a reason: They keep us safe on the road and prevent us from crashing into oncoming traffic. Without boundary lines in our own lives, our competing priorities are inevitably going to crash.

Boundaries are huge. I've seen the damage lack of boundaries causes to both individuals and organizations when people don't know what is and isn't theirs to focus on. Ultimately, a lack of clarity around boundaries leads to the inability to focus and negatively impacts the effectiveness of an organization.

Without clear boundaries, we won't succeed professionally or personally. It's up to each of us to know what's important to us, how to prioritize those things, how to stop doing what isn't important to us, and how to say "no" to things that other people think are important but don't really fit into our job description or life plan. We can't expect others to just "know" what we need. We have to tell them by setting clear boundaries.

But clear boundaries aren't any good if they're not enforced. We often set boundaries ("I'm not going to schedule anything this weekend," "I'm not going to watch TV after 9 p.m.") but then are surprised when we actually have to adhere to the boundary we set. Or we're caught off guard when someone else doesn't like our boundary ("Please, just one more episode?").

Boundaries are good, but the real magic comes when we enforce them.

And that takes discipline. It takes time to strengthen those boundary muscles. Just like it gets easier to hit the gym the more consistently you show up, enforcing boundaries becomes second nature the longer you're at it. Don't give up! Keep setting, communicating, enforcing, and reevaluating your boundaries until they're so ingrained in your workday that you don't even have to think about them!

I'm really clear on my values and my definition of success. I've spent time defining them, seeing how they influence my decisions, and seeing where I need to make different decisions to be more in alignment. If I didn't know my values or definition of success, I wouldn't know how or where to set boundaries. And I don't just mean success like professional success. I use success as a proxy for *What do I want for my life? Who do I want in it? What kind of relationships do I want? What are my long-term goals?* If you're unsure of the answers to these questions for yourself, a good place to start is with the Core Values Exercise in the Appendix. Clarify your values, and the boundaries you need to set will become clearer, too.

PRIORITIZE, MINIMIZE, DELEGATE

So far, I have identified my non-negotiables. I have created boundaries that protect those non-negotiables using methods like Core Hours and giving myself time to get into flow. But I still face the ongoing need to choose which tasks should get done first, and for how long.

We know it's impossible to work well and live well if we're trying to do it all. But how do we sift through our mountain of commitments and ever-growing list of to-dos? Is it possible to simplify decision-making and figure out what to say "no" to, so we can say "yes" to doing our best work without sacrificing other priorities?

Yes! To do that, I employ and advocate for a three-step system we call *Prioritize, Minimize, Delegate.*

Step 1: Prioritize

The biggest enemy of effectiveness is a lack of focus created by a confusion of competing priorities. And the enemy of prioritization might surprise you: it's *too many priorities.*

In fact, it's possible we've completely misunderstood the concept of prioritizing. The word "priorities" itself is a misnomer. Consider how the Oxford and Webster dictionaries define the word:

> "The fact or condition of being regarded or treated as more important than others."

> "Something given or meriting attention before competing alternatives."

Did you catch it? The definitions are singular in nature. These aren't definitions for the word *priorities*, they are definitions for the word *priority*, singular. And that tiny change makes a big difference.

You can't actually have more than one priority. Which means when it comes to setting priorities at work, you have to pick just one at a time— what we often refer to as our "top priority." If you want to priority-set correctly, your list should be short: just one most important thing. This takes the place of a long to-do list with dozens of priorities.

Of course, we don't live in a world where we typically have the luxury of focusing on just *one* thing, but that doesn't mean we shouldn't rethink how we priority-set. The idea is to stop the task-switching so many of us default to.

For example, we take a family trip to my hometown in northeastern Pennsylvania every summer. A few years ago, I asked the kids what their one priority was for our trip. They all had different answers: Jack wanted to fish, Everett wanted to play video games at the arcade, Elena didn't want to miss the county fair, and Dorothea wanted to go horseback riding. My husband and I also picked our top priority: him, swimming at our friend's pond and me, floating on the Delaware River.

In reality, we all wanted to do all of these things and more, but it was helpful to know what was most important to each person, so we could prioritize accordingly. And when someone said they wanted to do something else, we kindly asked, "*Is that more important to you than 'X'?*" That question drove the point home—we can't do everything. The result? Everyone felt heard, and everyone left feeling like they got what they wanted out of the trip.

If only one thing can be your top priority at one time, ask yourself: *What is **most** important to me?* What one thing needs to be done first? What is the most critical to your success that day, week, month, or year? That's your priority. Most times, our scattered priorities are revealed in our actions, and we're left feeling like we didn't actually accomplish what we wanted to do in a given day. Unless you understand your top priority, you're much less likely to achieve it.

That's why the first step in the Prioritize, Minimize, Delegate process is to list all the things on your to-do list. Yes, all of them! This may take some time, but seeing the full list of everything on your plate gives you the information you need to make decisions about what to accomplish when and what you need to delay, or simply delete. We'll include exercises for each step below to help you jumpstart the process.

EXERCISE: PRIORITIZE

Grab a piece of paper (or open a blank document) and download everything on your to-do list. It may help to divide this up into daily, weekly, and monthly tasks. Then rank them in order of importance, such as on a scale of 1-3: 1 for non-negotiables, 2 for things that should happen (but the world won't end if they don't), and 3 for "nice to-dos" but not necessary.

Step 2: Minimize

This is where the hard work begins. See that long list, ranked from highest priority to lowest? It's time to cross some things off. Chances are, you're doing more than you need to or more than you realistically can. Are there things on the list you've taken on that aren't helping you work well or live well anymore, like a standing meeting that can easily be an email? Or a social commitment you can return to at a different time when your priorities shift?

EXERCISE: MINIMIZE

Start slashing that list! Which to-dos fall into the lower third of your full list (aka the lowest priorities)? Cross them off! I wrote a cheeky article called "The Life-Changing Magic of Tidying Up Your Workday" you can find on the Thrive Global platform, founded by Ariana Huffington. It's a play on Marie Kondo's book, and follows the same steps to let go of things in your life, and on your to-do list, that no longer serve you.

Step 3: Delegate

Once you've cut down your to-do list by getting rid of the things that aren't helping you work well or live well, you can more clearly see your most pressing tasks. Now, the final step: delegate. Delegation is easier said than done. We often feel like we can do things better ourselves, or don't want to make the effort of passing something off. And of course there are the financial resources required for outsourcing. But delegation can prevent burnout, scale your organization for growth, and set an example of healthy work-life balance. Delegation is almost always a component of a sustainable pace.

EXERCISE: DELEGATE

To make delegation easier, we've created a Delegation Matrix. Use this box to list out all your responsibilities (it may be easier to create one for work and one for personal), adding more lines as needed. (You'll find a full-size matrix you can copy and use repeatedly in the Appendix.)

- Box 4: In the top right corner, list everything you love doing and are great at.

- Box 3: List the things you love but someone else could do better.

- Box 2: List things you're good at but don't enjoy.

- Box 1: List those tasks and responsibilities you neither enjoy or are good at.

- Finally, start delegating, beginning with the tasks listed in Box 1!

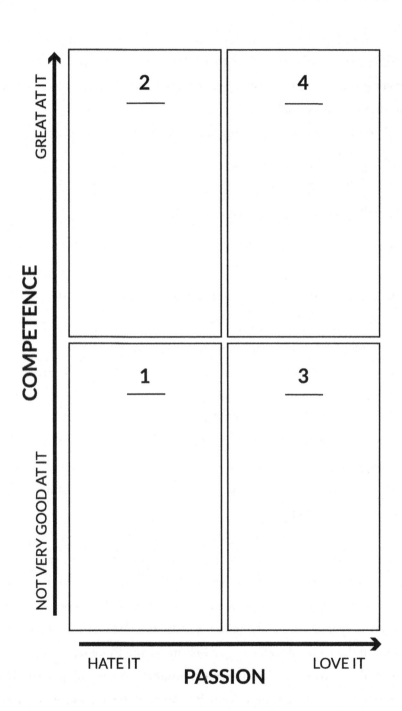

For high capacity individuals, it can be difficult to find responsibilities and tasks that fit in Boxes 1 through 3. Whether you truly love what you do or you have honed a skill set that sets you apart, letting go of even mundane, time-draining tasks can be hard.

Consider using the following questions to determine what is worth keeping and what can truly be delegated:

- Of all the things you're good at, what is the most personally fulfilling?

- What are you good at that others aren't as good at?

- What are you good at but someone else in the organization is equally good (or good enough) at?

- Of all the things you're good at, what has the highest ROI? (Hint: Anything with a lower ROI should be delegated or outsourced.)

Consider listing the responsibilities and tasks in Box 4 in order of highest ROI to lowest. Determine a reasonable number of responsibilities to leave in Box 4 based on your capacity (make sure you truly are reasonable!) and move the other tasks to Boxes 2 and 3.

We know this isn't an easy process for high-performing individuals, so start small. Delegate just one small task, see how it goes, and build a habit of trusting others to take on tasks that free you to do your most important work. Practice makes perfect!

And if that isn't motivation enough, MatchPace offers a *Delegation Protocol*. The protocol is a series of questions you make sure *you* answer *before* asking someone to take something off of your plate. You don't have to include this template in your request, but… you could! You can find the Delegation Protocol along the full-size Delegation Matrix to complete for yourself in the Appendix and on our website on the Resources page.

Finally, remember that the most important part of prioritizing, minimizing, and delegating is knowing yourself, having clarity on your

priorities, and being so committed to them that you're willing to let go of less important things.

Overcommitting ourselves is often an indication of lack of clarity or a sign of fear. We try using "hacks" to avoid the hard work of clarifying our priorities, and we cling to being too busy because we're scared to actually pursue the things most important to us. Or we fill every moment of our day to avoid actually sitting with ourselves, always needing the constant distraction of something keeping us from acknowledging our feelings. But hacks and over-scheduling ourselves never help us overcome our fears. Instead, they just serve as noise, distracting us from the real issues we must dig through. Only through self-awareness and acceptance can we dismantle our fear and improve our lives.

COUNTING THE COSTS

I preach pretty well about making hard choices and saying no. But when I try to implement it in my own life, I'm surprised when I'm disappointed with the outcomes.

Here's what I mean: When I prioritize my family and my business, I'm disappointed I don't have closer friendships. I get jealous when I see people spending time with each other on social media and I wasn't included. Similarly, while I have explicitly chosen to not exercise to the degree I used to, I'm disappointed I don't have the level of fitness I used to experience.

I wish I had a better pep talk to get us all through the downsides, but really, I think it's a matter of counting the costs.

It seems important to point out here that saying "no" doesn't mean you magically don't care about what you said "no" to. It's not as if taking things off your list means never thinking of them again or never feeling regret. That's just not the case. It's a little like forgiveness—forgiving the debt someone else caused you does come with a cost, even if it's the right thing to do. You still face consequences, even if the consequences aren't your fault.

You pay the cost of saying no. And sometimes that cost is hard to bear. Does it mean you made the wrong decision? Not necessarily. But pretending that there's no cost to saying "no" isn't a realistic picture to paint. There are almost always downsides to making wise choices—saying "no" is no exception. This has certainly been the case for me in every stage of life.

Does thinking through the downsides of saying "no" in order to combat and prevent burnout make you feel like it might not be worth it—like you may want to take the risk of burning out or just muscle your way through?

When you consider your professional life as a marathon that will likely last decades, pace becomes incredibly important, and dealing with the downsides of saying "no" so that you can run at a healthy, sustainable pace is a small price to pay for long-term wellness and professional success.

CHAPTER 10

REIMAGINING THE SYSTEM

A ND NOW WE'VE ARRIVED AT THE FINAL CONCENTRIC circle: Systemic Pace, or the pace set by the systems within our society and culture. While we can all take great strides toward a more sustainable pace for ourselves and our organizations using the strategies outlined in this book, we can't fully reimagine the workday without first reimagining the systems within which we work.

In this chapter I unpack some of the ways our systems make a sustainable pace difficult, if not impossible, for many people in our society. Some of what I say might seem like a no-brainer, and other facts and ideas may make you squirm. That's okay. Unless we are all committed to setting a sustainable pace for *everyone*, none of us will truly be able to work well and live well.

As I mentioned earlier in the book, we're no longer living in the Industrial Age. Our economy now revolves around knowledge and information and is largely dictated by so-called "white-collar" jobs. In this economy, the most valuable assets aren't assembly lines but our brains. Management expert Peter Drucker anticipated this shift, and world-renowned futurists Alvin and Heidi Toffler wrote extensively about what they termed the "Third Wave." Their work foreshadowed some of the sweeping effects of rapid technology development on people, businesses, and government.

As a consultant with Toffler Associates, a management consulting firm rooted in the ideas and methodologies of the Tofflers, and later, as a financial manager within a Fortune 500 company, I had the opportunity to help organizations through this transition to a more heavily knowledge-based approach. These roles shaped my thinking about how the world works and gave me insight into both the benefits and challenges of our knowledge and capitalist economy.

One thing our knowledge economy has in common with the Industrial Age? Capitalism. With the innovation and funds that capitalism unlocks come more than a few strings, including the quarterly earnings drumbeat. When it's unchecked, capitalism sets an inherent pace for all of us that prioritizes financial profit and results in financial gain and power for the few "at the top."

How does this tie to our pace? Our workday is driven by the pursuit of positive quarterly earnings reports. Earnings statements often reward fast wins—not necessarily good work or creative work (though those things are sometimes rewarded), but instead, who can create a quick impact that maximizes profits. It sets a relentless pace that only the few who are singularly focused on work can sustain. Historically, primarily one group of people has been able to provide that singular focus and reap the rewards: white men. As a result, women and people of color do not always benefit from the capitalist market, and the organizations they participate in don't always benefit from the creativity and capabilities these people could bring to the marketplace.

While we've talked a lot about the *why* of a sustainable, matched pace and the *how* behind setting a sustainable pace for yourself and your organization, it's no use reimagining our workday unless we also reimagine the system within which our workday exists—that largest concentric circle. When I reimagine the system, I quickly realize what many construction companies know so well: a new build is easier than a renovation. And though that may be true, easy just isn't always an option. Remember my net-zero house I mentioned in Chapter 1? Well, that house was 80 years old. When my spouse and I decided to ensure our house produced more energy than it consumed, virtually all of the examples we had were brand-new builds. We could either defeatedly accept that it just wasn't possible, or we could be determined to make it work.

It requires clear diagnoses and strategic blueprints to enhance equity and justice for all and to give opportunity to all employees. When we talk about equity in the workplace, we're talking about a workplace that works for everyone. Unfortunately, that's not the world in which we work. Our current systems, from our economy on down to systems of rewards and advancement within organizations, benefit some people much more than others.

There is a critical relationship between equity and pace. In an economy driven primarily by growth and profits, where only those who can give *everything* rise to the top, how can organizations set a sustainable working pace that empowers all employees to contribute, succeed, be fairly compensated, and also have time for their other priorities?

First, let's look at how the current pace of work impacts people of different identities.

Gender

A common explanation for the existing gender pay gap (which sits at women making an average of $0.81 for every dollar earned by men[24]) is due to women's caretaking responsibilities. Women are often seen to be less committed to their careers because they take maternity leave, simply take more time off work, or request part-time schedules so they can accommodate their families' needs.

The gender pay gap grows when you add in race (an issue of intersectionality we'll discuss shortly). Black women on average make $0.63 cents on the dollar compared to men; Indigenous women make $0.60 and Latina women make $0.55 for every dollar made by men. Issues of gender, race, and economic justice are complicated, but these stats alone speak to the grave importance of pursuing a just working pace for all people.

While policies that enforce pay equity are important, consider this: Given all the inefficiencies and waste in a traditional workday, if you instead eliminate that waste for *everyone*, no one would have to work extra-long hours to prove their worth. **Our current systems reward people who have more time to waste.**

For example, in a heterosexual couple, a man may be able to stay late at the office while his wife does school pick-up, which has the male partner *looking* more committed to his work. To his bosses, his long hours demonstrate his commitment level, even if he simply wasted his afternoon and is making up for it after hours. On the other hand, employers may be more likely to assume a working mother is uncommitted and distracted. Leaving on time to pick up her children can be interpreted that her focus seems to be more on her kids than her work, even if she simply focused enough to finish all her work.

If we move away from a system that rewards more hours at a desk and instead focuses on what a person actually produces, we can make great strides toward recognizing women's contributions in the workplace and closing the gender pay gap. At MatchPace, we call this change in productivity measurement: *outcome-focused work*.

Parental Status

I once read the blog of a "productivity guru,", and he shared the story of how he proudly gave his wife $20 to go have coffee with her friends when she was 38 weeks pregnant. Her nesting (a common desire to clean and organize leading up to a baby's birth) was interfering with the project he was working on, and he wanted time alone to work. If that doesn't land with you right away, pause here and realize that the person who didn't have the burden (and good fortune) of carrying their child could "shoo away" the person who did because the caretaking for their unborn child was interfering with his focus.

I read another productivity book where the author, a father, used himself as an example: He closes his door every morning for several hours until he's done with his main work. As I mentioned above, I think blocking off several hours on a regular basis is a great idea—as long as someone else is making sure the kids get out the door for school, letting the dog out to go to the bathroom, managing home-related appointments, and acting as a gatekeeper for all things so you can work uninterrupted.

And those are both examples of inequity from two-parent households. Single parents face an even larger challenge without someone to share the caregiving responsibilities.

When we focus on relentless work and producing more and more in a professional or financial sense, we devalue the attention that is needed to be present with children and other family members outside of work—ensuring our health as a society. I know there are plenty of surveys that argue mothers spend more time with their children than they have in the past, but both research, and my own life, show that time is rarely spent being present, and more about "family logistics" (the meal prep, cleanup, laundry, etc. required to keep a family going). And our family doesn't even do extracurricular activities—I'm not in my chauffeur stage of parenting yet!

If we shift our professional focus from trying to conquer the world to trying to flourish as a human race and work at a more sustainable pace, we can be more present and engaged with our families, which—for most of us—will be the one of the deepest impacts we make in the world.

Racial Identity

In the last few years, attention to the deep-seated issues of systemic racism and injustice that still exist in the United States has grown. That, of course, extends to systemic racism in the workplace.

The fact is, Black people in the United States have suffered from centuries of "unprecedented levels of unregulated and unrestrained violences directed at them," as Cornel West explains in his book, *Race Matters.* They've experienced psychic violence, physical violence, weathering (poor health outcomes due to generations of violence and stress), and, of course, the exploitation of their labor.

We can't create workplaces that give people permission to work well and live well if people of all races are not able to work at a sustainable, just pace. We must address underlying issues stemming from the violence experienced by non-white workers, particularly the centuries of stolen resources (labor, land, emotional and intellectual capital) from Black and Indigeneous people.

We see the economic injustice of systemic racism starkly when we look at the racial wealth gap. A report released in 2018 found that the median Black household has *less than 11 percent of the wealth* of the median white household.[25]

Lack of household wealth means marginalized families may not have savings and other assets to fall back on in times of economic hardship. They may not have college savings accounts to provide their children with opportunities for higher education. Marginalized people are less likely to own homes, often leading to housing instability. All of these factors and more add up to a completely different paradigm when approaching work: Instead of focusing on climbing the career ladder, many families are simply trying to pay their bills, paycheck to paycheck. It's a lot easier to work an an unpaid internship when you don't have to work at a job to pay for your living expenses; it's easier to be more prepared for a job interview when you got a good night's sleep, which is hard to do when you had to work late or live in a home that doesn't have dependable climate control.

This means that sometimes marginalized people aren't even on the corporate ladder. For many, due to circumstances way beyond their control, they simply cannot keep up the pace in a white-collar knowledge economy. Not only is our current professional system dehumanizing, our organizations are missing out on the talent, creativity, and diversity of perspective that is necessary for true organizational success. Until we reconcile our working pace so that all races have a chance to grow professionally, we all suffer.

Socioeconomic Status

In our profit-driven knowledge economy, salaried employees are perceived to have more value than hourly employees, just like full-time employees are thought (however subconsciously) to be more valuable than part-time employees, even if the part-time employee produces exceptionally high-quality work. Those who have to—or choose to—work less have fewer opportunities for advancement as well.

We've looked at those at the top—mostly white men (and occasionally, white women), with the ability to give much of their time, energy, and attention to their work because they have a network of support around them (spouses, childcare, household help, etc.) to make that possible and ensure they stay at the top. When someone is further "down" the socioeconomic ladder, the further from reach that kind of support gets—without additional funds to pay for extended childcare or the ability to outsource household responsibilities—and the greater the inability to "keep up" at our socially-dictated pace. Similarly, hourly workers are typically the lowest paid and also have little to no flexibility or paid time off to accommodate other needs, such as a sick child, a benefit that usually only comes with a full-time, salaried, information-based position.

In an information-based job, an employer pays for value, not necessarily hours put in (even though we structure our workday by hours). By nature of how our current systems view the value of skilled worker jobs (colloquially called blue-collar, pink-collar, or no-collar jobs) are disproportionately held by women and people of color who have historically been marginalized— these workers are often hesitant to ascribe higher financial value to their work by asking for raises or benefits. **That leaves them needing to work more to make more, and at a disadvantage when it comes to living at a sustainable pace.**

Example in point: We moved out of our net-zero house and into a new house a few years ago, and the gentleman who mowed the lawn for the previous owners asked if we wanted him to mow for us. We had a four-year-old, a three-year-old and one-year-old twins... who were we kidding? We could barely brush our teeth and needed all the help we could get–we said "yes."

The previous owner had done a unique (read: odd) thing in the yard: To delineate a garden, he drilled over thirty, three-and-a-half foot metal poles into the ground and put bricks atop the six inches of pole sticking out above the ground. We wanted to remove it all.

Andy and I spent two hours one evening trying to dig some of the poles out; we removed three of them. That was about four man-hours of our time (we were also playing with our kids, so definitely not four focused hours, but any future hours working on this wouldn't be either). In defeat, we asked the man who mowed our lawn if he could help us. There were 30+ stakes in the ground and he had them out in 30 minutes. His lifetime of lawn care experience gave him an understanding of torque, and with a 2x4 and a strap, he leveraged them out like he was pulling carrots out of the garden.

He thought of the value of his work as hourly—the couple of minutes it took him to take the poles out—so he sheepishly charged us $20. But the value to us was much greater, and we paid him according to that value. This is just one example of how critical the shift toward paying people for the value they provide is, even when (and perhaps, especially when) their work has been historically undervalued.

Disability

There are different types of disabilities: physical, cognitive, sensory, mental health, and learning disabilities. Disability is a very collective label that covers a huge range of experiences and needs.

Challenges for people with disabilities in the workplace often start with entering (and remaining) in the workforce in the first place. The Organization for Economic Cooperation and Development, a non-profit organization that works to set international standards for social, economic, and environmental challenges, reports that the employment rate for people with disabilities is around 40%, compared to 75% for people without a disability.[26]

Creating an environment where people with disabilities can work, let alone work well, takes intentionality and effort. Something that has stood out to me as I've learned about the disability community through friends and through reading is the difference between the Medical Model and the Social Model. Here's a very basic explanation: The Medical Model focuses on the limitations of a person's disabilities and how you can correct, cure, or eliminate their disabilities. The Social Model focuses not on "fixing" a person with disabilities but instead changing our society to create opportunities for them. Instead of eliminating functional impairments this model seeks to improve a person's daily function in society.

In fact, the Social Model can and should be applied to all of our conversations around diversity. For so long, our societal approach has been to try to change or "fix" the things that make someone different. But if we can instead shift our societal structures to make room for more people at the table as they are, we'll truly benefit from the diverse experiences and perspectives they bring.

Intersectionality

Gender, race, sex, sexuality, religion, disability, age, parental status, and economic status are all intermingled when we look at how the current pace of industry, and primarily the knowledge-based economy, functions. Minoritized people in any one category, or a combination of several, are subjugated by our systems in different ways, and the results (like the racial wealth gap, the gender pay gap, and the gap in leadership diversity) are robbing talented, hard-working individuals of the opportunity to rise "to the top" in an economy dictated by an unsustainable pace.

Kimberlé Crenshaw, a lawyer, college professor, and advocate, originated the term *intersectionality*. The term, according to her 1989 paper "Demarginalizing the Intersection of Race and Sex", is the tendency to treat race and gender (and other identities) as mutually exclusive categories of experience. This tendency marginalizes those who are multiply-burdened and obscures claims that cannot be understood as resulting from single sources of discrimination.[27] People's "intersecting identities" mean that they are impacted by systems and injustices in ways you can't see if you just look at one identity or one form of discrimination. Intersectionality affects our ability to achieve a sustainable pace at work. It's one thing for a woman to try to achieve a sustainable pace at work; it's another thing for a single mother to try to achieve a sustainable pace, and another thing entirely for a black single mother to try to achieve a sustainable pace. The multiple layers of a person's identity impact them differently in their quest for a meaningful professional pace, and all of these layers need to be acknowledged.

Joy in Equity

Yes, there is weight when we consider diversity, equity, and inclusion. But if we look for it, there is also a lightness. I have been privileged to experience multiple cultures other than my own. My family hosted exchange students when I was growing up, and I have "siblings" in several other countries. I was welcomed into families' homes in Thailand as a 17-year-old exchange student myself where I got to go to a Thai high school, make friends, and learn to cook Thai food (lucky me!). The Step Team at the University of New Mexico (UNM) welcomed me with open arms when a friend invited me to a practice, dinner after practice, and practice the next week. Another fellow student at UNM invited me to his home on the Navajo Nation for some of his community's celebrations. I had the privilege to watch a colleague blossom into themselves when they transitioned from their gender assigned at birth to their true gender identity. When I lived in the Philippines, I had the opportunity to volunteer at a ministry dedicated to the wellbeing of Filipino street children—the delight I experienced while participating in their lives is still so strong inside of my heart.

Foods, sounds, textures, languages, smells—it is absolutely beautiful to consider the variety of people, perspectives, and experiences around the world.

Advocating for diverse inclusion and equitable living in the world is not a burden. It is an honor to know and be known by people who have lived lives different than our own. The benefit to our workplace is both incalculable and measurable: increased creativity and innovation, increased employee engagement, and increased revenue and profit. In a study by the Boston Consulting Group (BCG), the researchers found that "increasing the diversity of leadership teams leads to more and better innovation and improved financial performance"—on average with a 19% increase in revenue.[28]

When we are singularly focused on productivity, we're moving too hard and fast to notice others, and we miss the *joy* of working together.

At MatchPace, our values are *working well and living well*—or maybe that's actually one value. Because it's the combination of those two things that make life valuable for us. Work is important. When people bring their best creativity to work, they solve the world's problems and create a better world. Work provides income for people to support and spend time with their families. And people need to be able to live well - to have deep relationships, to be connected to their communities, to have access to health and support.

Work only works when it works for everyone—when it is just.

Equity, Justice & Pace

How can we address systemic injustice in our economic system with a better pace? We can start by recognizing that everyone's work plays a crucial role in our functioning as a society. *All* work has value. Teachers, administrative assistants, sanitation workers, nurses, marketing executives, retail workers, CEOs—we all play a vital role in our economy. I dare you to reimagine a workforce that rewards work based on the value it brings to society, not how much profit it generates for shareholders.

These systemic issues are why we work with *organizations* and the people who lead them, instead of focusing primarily on individual employees. We truly feel for people who are burned out—we ourselves have been there, and we want to see burnout become a non-issue for all workers, from the C-suite to the hourly wage earner. If you're currently suffering from burnout from any of the factors listed previously—or any reason at all—we hope this book helps you figure out some ways to reverse burnout and find more clarity and focus in your work.

And, only addressing an individual and their symptoms and causes of burnout is a bit like telling someone to take a bubble bath or "just say no" when they're drowning in absolute overwhelm. It's, um... nice. While a break is often a welcome change of pace, a short break doesn't solve the real problem: oppressive work environments.

My husband and I actually have a 'shorthand' for this concept. There's a verse in the Bible, James 2:16, that says, "*If one of you says to him, "Go, I wish you well; keep warm and well fed," but does nothing about his physical needs, what good is it? In the same way, faith by itself, if it is not accompanied by action, is dead."* When we hear someone suggest a band-aid fix for burnout, we'll give each other a sideways glance and say, "Be warm and well fed!" What we really mean is, "That's nice–but won't actually solve the problem."

We need systemic change in our society. And of course, there's the corresponding Work^Power of systemic change. Work^1 looks like someone (the law, your boss, etc.) telling you that you need to have diversity on your team, so you hire someone. Or at an organizational level, you need to follow Affirmative Action hiring practices. At first it's just something you have to do. Then you start to notice the changes it brings to your team— that people who are different from you and the majority of your teammates have a different perspective, and that perspective refines your work and makes it better. That is Work^2.

But true systemic change comes from leaders doing Work^3. It's a result of deep, sustaining, individual change from those who are leading our organizations. That's why we prioritize coaching—executive coaching is included in each of our engagements because we know how important it is for leaders to come to an understanding about themselves and make critical transitions (Work^3). Coaching is a guided practice of self-examination, where the coach supports the individual to maximize their personal and professional growth. I had the privilege to attend the Coach Diversity Institute with Dr. Towanna Burrous, where I developed the skills to help leaders create transformation in their organizations without skirting around the issues of power and privilege that underpin the challenges so much of our community faces. My training taught me how to help leaders face issues surrounding race, ethnicity, culture, religion, sexual orientation, and ability head-on, all of which have a personal impact on their lives, as well as the lives of those in their organizations.

Their change will expand to how organizations work and address the systemic inequities that keep people marginalized. We need practical changes to address the mental load of people who struggle under multiple systems that are ultimately designed to keep them oppressed.

A bubble bath or "just saying no" is fine for a bit of breathing room, but we are seeking *workplace justice*. And that is going to come from changing the systems we work in.

We must reshape our culture to stop valuing full-time, salaried, knowledge work over part-time or hourly labor. This book is not about advocating specific policy solutions, but it should go without saying that shifting work culture is tied to work policies. Our aim is to simply reward effective work that adds value to our society. Reimagining the workday is ultimately an issue of equity and justice, so that *all* employees—regardless of their job type, and regardless of their identities—can work at a sustainable pace. This may be one of the more difficult and uncomfortable ways you are being asked to reimagine your workday, but one that is infinitely worth the work it will take to get there.

CONCLUSION

DON'T FORGET
WHAT'S AT STAKE

———

THE WAY WE'RE WORKING ISN'T WORKING. BUT WE believe the concepts introduced in this book should give us all hope because it *is* possible to work well, make the most of our time, and leave our workday behind us with a sense of accomplishment as we turn our focus toward our many other priorities.

We began our journey toward effectiveness with the foundational idea that good work matters. We often take the concept of work for granted: We work to put food on the table, to fill our time, to make enough money to do all the other things we want to do. But work has intrinsic value by itself—bringing purpose and meaning to our lives and offering solutions to problems our society faces. Through our work we not only contribute to the flourishing of ourselves and our families, we also contribute to our communities and society as a whole. Good work matters.

We've suffered as work has taken up a disproportionate amount of time, and even value, in our lives. Many have given their lives over to their work, sacrificing all other elements of who they are: fellow human, neighbor, friend, sibling, partner, parent, person with interests and hobbies. It's time to bring our pace at work into alignment with our whole selves, working in a way that empowers us as we participate in solving the very real challenges facing our world today—*without* causing harm to our bodies, relationships, and planet.

Work is how we solve every problem we face as a human race, but it's also (often) how we create more problems. It doesn't have to be that way. Using the tools in this book to discover and set a sustainable pace for yourself and your organization is a first, small step toward bringing work back into alignment with everything around us. Establishing a healthy pace at work has a domino effect of improving the health of our bodies, minds, relationships, and communities.

These days, as I give my time, effort, and energy to building a business, raising four children, and being an engaged citizen, running triathlons just isn't a priority. My current pace dictates less pushing and more tending to not just my physical needs but my mental and emotional needs as well. Is there another triathlon in my future? Maybe! But staying true to a sustainable pace in this season of my life means prioritizing differently, pushing in different areas and resting in others. This is how I feel fully human.

What I'm really advocating for—as I nudge you toward a healthy, sustainable working pace—is *reclaiming our humanity in the workplace*. If the COVID-19 pandemic revealed anything, it's how interconnected we all are and how we've forgotten we bring our whole selves to work. We don't leave our roles behind when we punch the proverbial clock. It's when we forget we are real people, working with real people, that we set the stage for overwhelm and burnout.

While restoring humanity in the workplace is worth an entire book itself, there are a few things I encourage you to keep in mind as you pursue a sustainable working pace for yourself and your organization. If your career is a marathon during which it's critical to pace ourselves, you cannot forget that we're running alongside others. You want *everyone* to successfully finish the race with their whole selves intact.

First, we can't neglect our own mental health or the mental health of our colleagues, employees, and leaders. It sounds cheesy, but we lose our humanity when we prioritize productivity over compassion. Yes, work needs to get done, and good work—absolutely. I hope it's clear how much I value work and how grateful I am for the businesses, non-profits, and government organizations that provide for us. But when we bring our whole selves to work, we bring our anxiety, grief, exhaustion, and fear to work, too. It became hard to dismiss the mental and emotional health of workers during COVID-19, as the entire world faced the chaos and uncertainty of the virus. Can we carry that same sensitivity and compassion into a post-COVID world, too?

While having a clear mission, communicating shared values, and implementing norms that reflect those values all go a long way toward helping your team set and maintain a sustainable pace at work, I also want to ask you to think through how you want to respond to the real human concerns your team members will face throughout their tenure at your organization. How do you want people to interact with each other? Will you prioritize compassion and kindness over productivity? Is it more important to the leaders of your organization to win the race or to make it across the finish line together?

Finally, don't forget that you can take the concept of pace and apply it in every area of your life. While work is often the primary source of burnout in our lives, it's far from the only one. If you're a caregiver, you may be feeling burned out as you meet the demands of those dependent on you. Putting your needs aside to meet theirs will lead to burnout if you don't find a way to balance your health with theirs. If you're active and engaged in your community, you may find public service asks for more than you can realistically give while you maintain your mental, emotional, and physical health.

Our many roles and priorities make us who we are and give our lives meaning, but when we're running at an unsustainable pace in one area, we end up out of balance and metaphorically (or literally) injured—physically, mentally, and emotionally. Working at a sustainable pace is so intertwined with *living* at a sustainable pace—and that is the foundation for a successful life.

Before you go, please remember that in the Appendix you will find exercises that you can use as you set your own sustainable pace, from defining your values to discovering your ideal schedule based on your ChronoPace and learning to Prioritize, Minimize, and Delegate. These exercises pertain not just to your work but also how you engage with your family, hobbies, community, and rest. Learn to apply the concepts of pace to your whole self.

It should be clear by now that more is at stake than just your bottom line when it comes to helping your organization work at a sustainable pace. Pace is the difference between an organization that retains highly engaged talent and one that burns employees out. It's the difference between a work environment that empowers employees to thrive versus one where everyone is just surviving. It's the difference between a workplace that honors and values the humanity of every worker and one that treats them like expendable commodities.

So, what is the future of work? Ultimately, we don't know what work will look like one, five, or 10 years from now—and that's ok. The beauty of pace is that it doesn't have to—and shouldn't—stay the same forever. The pace of your organization and your pace as an individual can and will speed up or slow down at different points in time. Reevaluating the pace at which you work on a regular basis allows you to remain agile in the face of constant change.

Nobody knows what the future of work will look like, but we all have the opportunity to create it. My hope is that we will choose to use this time to reimagine how we work as individuals, organizations, and whole societies. It's time to prioritize a sustainable pace at work and create a better future for all of us—at work and beyond.

Working well *and* living well is possible. Discover which pace works for you and your organization, commit to it, and achieve professional success that honors and serves your whole self, your family, your community, and our world. *That* is good work.

APPENDIX

CORE HOUR
STRUCTURE SAMPLES

S AMPLE A: A NON-PROFIT CONSULTING TEAM, WITH
the team located on the East Coast and clients
around the country

- Meetings: meetings can *only* be scheduled between 10 a.m. E and 4
  p.m. E to start the week with a focused block of time for work, and
  protect the beginning and the end of the day for deep focus (providing both Early and Mid-Morning and Afternoon/Evening Pacers
  appropriate focus blocks)

- In Office: Each week all staff are in the office on Mondays, Tuesdays,
  Wednesdays and Thursdays during the prescribed meeting hours
  to enable in-person collaborative work (unless traveling for client
  needs), with some staff working at home all or part of the remaining
  days/times of the week

- Weekly focus day: No meetings *at all (team or client)* on Fridays - the team can work in the office or remotely
- Monthly:
  - The first Tuesday of every month is an "all hands on deck" day, when everyone is definitely in the office (they carefully don't schedule work travel for that day/week) the team prioritizes administrative tasks (like all-staff training, booking travel for the month, etc).
  - All staff are empowered to schedule a monthly "airplane day" when they are working, but without interruption. Airplane days are scheduled in advance, so other meetings can be scheduled around them.

Sample B: a small for-profit company with teammates across the country, providing client services to companies across the country (all teammates work out of their homes, with some travel to client sites)

- Meetings: client meetings are targeted to Mondays through Wednesdays, between 11 a.m. ET and 6 p.m. ET to be available to clients in different time zones but still respect reasonable start/end times for teammates
- In Office: N/A
- Weekly focus days: No meetings at all (team or client) on Thursdays
- Team collaboration day: team meetings are generally scheduled for Fridays (project team meetings, whole staff meetings, etc)
- Quarterly: the teams gather for two days in a new, fun location for team-building, training, and real-life problem solving. All teammates are expected to be present in-person.

DELEGATION MATRIX & DELEGATION PROTOCOL

———

WHETHER YOU'RE A ONE-PERSON SHOP OR LEADING a team, delegation is critical for success. Delegation can prevent burnout, scale your organization for growth, and set an example for healthy work-life balance. Here's how to sort through all of your roles and responsibilities and determine what should stay in your wheelhouse and what can be effectively delegated.

Use the matrix on the next page to list out all of your roles and responsibilities, adding more lines as needed.

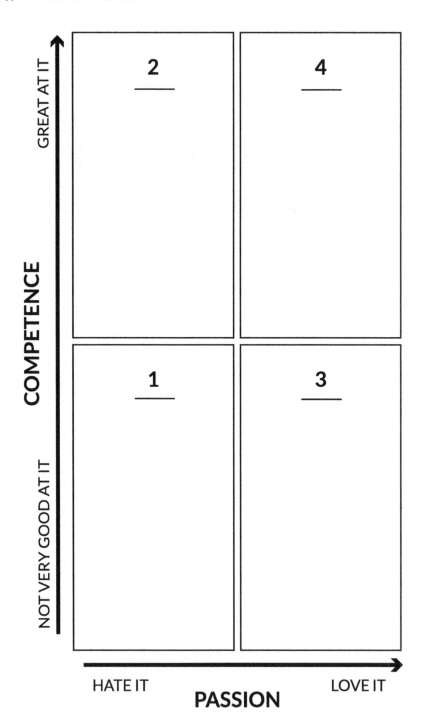

- Box 4: In the top right corner, list everything you love doing and are great at.

- Box 3: List the things you love but someone else could do better.

- Box 2: List things you're good at but don't enjoy.

- Box 1: List those tasks and responsibilities you neither enjoy or are good at.

- Finally, start delegating, beginning with the tasks listed in Box 1!

But what if you just don't know what to give up?

For high capacity individuals, it can be difficult to find responsibilities and tasks that fit in Boxes 1, 2 and 3. Whether you truly love what you do, or you have honed a skill set that sets you apart, letting go of even mundane, time-draining tasks can be hard.

Consider using the following questions to determine what is worth keeping and what can truly be delegated:

- Of all the things you're good at, what is the most personally fulfilling?

- What are you good at that others aren't as good at?

- What are you good at, but someone else in the organization is equally good (or good enough) at?

- Of all the things you're good at, what has the highest ROI? (Hint: Anything with a lower ROI should be delegated or outsourced.)

Consider listing the responsibilities and tasks in Box 4 in order of highest return to lowest. Determine a reasonable number of responsibilities to leave in Box 4 based on your own capacity (make sure you truly are reasonable!) and move the other tasks to Boxes 2 and 3. We know this isn't an easy process for high-performing individuals, so start small. Delegate just one small task, see how it goes, and build a habit of trusting others to take on tasks that free you to do your most important work. Try our delegation protocol below to outline clear communication and goal-setting as you delegate.

EXERCISE: DELEGATION PROTOCOL

- Name the person I'm delegating to:

- Clearly state the task:

- Clarify if I'm interested in them performing a process in a specific way or if I'm mainly interested in the outcome (ie: Do I want them to make a project budget? Or do I want them to use the standard template for a project budget? - there's a difference, make sure it's clear).

- Is there a timeline? Review periods? Deliverable date?

- What is the impact if the task is not completed?

- What accountability will there be if someone isn't making progress?

- Who else needs to know that you've delegated to this person? Who will need to take their guidance, or supply information to them?

- **Bold**, <u>underline</u>, *italicize* things you want to draw people's attention to:

  - If you're delegating via email, be super clear at the top of your email so people know what to look for:

    * ACTION for:

    * FYI for:

CORE VALUES EXERCISE

Step 1: Check up to 25 values that resonate with you.

☐ Abundance	☐ Fulfillment	☐ Popularity
☐ Acceptance	☐ Fun	☐ Power
☐ Accountability	☐ Genius	☐ Professional
☐ Achievement	☐ Growth	☐ Advancement
☐ Adventure	☐ Happiness	☐ Prosperity
☐ Art	☐ Honesty	☐ Reliability
☐ Balance	☐ Humor	☐ Reason
☐ Beauty	☐ Impact	☐ Recognition
☐ Calm	☐ Independence	☐ Relaxation
☐ Commitment	☐ Initiative	☐ Respect
☐ Communication	☐ Innovation	☐ Responsibility
☐ Community	☐ Integrity	☐ Safety
☐ Compassion	☐ Intelligence	☐ Security
☐ Competence	☐ Intuition	☐ Self-awareness
☐ Conflict Resolution	☐ Justice	☐ Self-mastery
☐ Connection	☐ Knowledge	☐ Social Change
☐ Courage	☐ Leadership	☐ Social Justice
☐ Creativity	☐ Learning	☐ Spirituality
☐ Creativity	☐ Love	☐ Stability
☐ Diversity	☐ Love	☐ Success
☐ Equity	☐ Loyalty	☐ Surrender
☐ Excellence	☐ Morals	☐ Teamwork
☐ Expression	☐ Nature	☐ Transparency
☐ Fairness	☐ Openness	☐ Truth-seeking
☐ Faith	☐ Order	☐ Understanding
☐ Fame	☐ Patience	☐ Variety
☐ Family	☐ Peace	☐ Vision
☐ Free Time	☐ Perseverance	☐ Wealth
☐ Freedom	☐ Personal Growth	☐ Well-being
☐ Friends	☐ Physical Wellness	☐ Wisdom

Step 2: Are any of the values you chose similar to each other? Group them together.

GROUP 1	GROUP 2	GROUP 3	GROUP 4

GROUP 5	GROUP 6	GROUP 7	GROUP 8

Step 3: Pick <u>one word</u> that represents the group

GROUP 1	GROUP 2	GROUP 3	GROUP 4

GROUP 5	GROUP 6	GROUP 7	GROUP 8

Step 4: Star the top 6

Step 5: List your top 4 values

Step 6: Add a verb to the top 4 (*Ex. Act with integrity*)

Step 7: Prioritize your core values. Ask yourself:
- **If I could only have 3 of these, which would I choose?**
- **If I could only have 2, which would I choose?**
- **If I could only have 1, which would I choose.**
Write them down in priority order.

Step 8: Post your core values in physical or virtual spaces!

SAMPLE CHRONOPACE SCHEDULES

SAMPLE EARLY MORNING SCHEDULE

Below is an example schedule for someone with an Early Morning Pacer. The times highlighted in gray are the peak performance times for Early Morning Pacers and the non-highlighted blocks are your non-peak hours. Time blocking is best done in 60 to 90 minute blocks to align with ultradian cycles.

4:00am - 5:00am	*Wakeup*
Wakeup - 6:30am	Plan your day and focus attention on the things that are most important to you. This may be a good time to meditate, journal, do focused work on a hobby, or start your most critical work for the day.
6:30am	Transition to the workday. Give your mind a chance to prepare for the day as you commute to the office or move into your workspace.
7:00am - 8:30am	This is a great time for analytical or strategic tasks. Prioritize tasks that require deep-focus and problem-solving.

8:30am	Take a short break before transitioning to another focused block. This is a great time for a short walk or to grab a coffee/snack.
8:45am - 10:00am	You are likely in your flow during this period. Continue working on analytical tasks and try to ensure any meetings/calls that you take during this period are ones where you are actively involved in thinking through processes or making decisions, and are not just status updates.
10:00am - 11:30am	This is a good time to catch up on administrative tasks. Check emails or participate in informational meetings.
11:30am - 12:30pm	Take a lunch break. If you can get outside and get a little sun it may be a good stimulant for your body to get through the afternoon when you will naturally be more tired. Even if you can't get outside, try to avoid having lunch in the same space where you work.
12:30pm - 2:00pm	This is a good time for more creative work. Your mind may start to wander but that may be needed for brainstorming or coming up with new ideas/ innovations.
2:00pm	Take a short break. Step away from your computer screen and do a breathing exercise to improve blood flow and increase your energy levels. This break may also be a good time to socialize with colleagues.
2:15pm - 4:00pm	This is a good time for administrative tasks like team meetings, preparing status updates for clients, and scheduling time for the next day. Time in this block is also well used to catch-up with co-workers as well as relationship building with colleagues and clients.

4:00pm - 5:00pm	Time to transition between professional and non-professional commitments is an important part of each day. Make sure to take the time you need to refill your tank to give your best to what is most important to you in your personal life.
5:00pm - 6:00pm	This is the best time of day for cardio or exercises like yoga, to increase flexibility.
6:00pm - 8:00pm	This is a great time for low impact socializing with friends or spending time with family. It is a good time for creative play.
8:00pm - 9:00pm	Relaxation before bed is key for you to get a good night sleep and thrive the next day. Unplug and keep things low key before bed.
9:00pm - 10:00pm	*Sleep Onset*

SAMPLE MID-MORNING SCHEDULE

Below is an example of the schedule of someone with a Mid-Morning Pacer. The times highlighted in gray are the peak performance times for Mid-Morning Pacers and the non-highlighted blocks are your non-peak hours. Time blocking is best done in 60 to 90 minute blocks to align with ultradian cycles.

5:30am - 6:30am	*Wakeup*
Wakeup - 7:00am	Take a few moments to ease into your day. Start your morning with a few deep breaths to improve blood flow and give you a small burst of energy. Eat a protein-rich breakfast. Open the curtains and get a little natural light, this will signal to your body that it is time to start the day.
7:00am - 8:00am	Transition to the workday. Give your mind a chance to prepare for the day as you commute to the office or move into your workspace.
8:00am - 9:30am	This is a great time for analytical or strategic tasks. Prioritize tasks that require deep-focus and problem-solving.
9:30am	Take a short break before transitioning to another focused block. This is a great time for a short walk or to meditate to sharpen your focus.
9:45am - 10:45am	You are likely in your flow during this period. Continue working on analytical tasks and try to ensure any meetings/calls that you take during this period are ones where you are actively involved in thinking through processes or making decisions, and are not just status updates.
10:45am	Take a short break from your computer screen to allow your eyes to relax.

10:45am - 12:00pm	This is a good time for you to develop strategy, do tasks that require problem-solving, or make difficult decisions.
12:00pm - 1:00pm	Take a lunch break. If you can get outside and get a little sun it may be a good stimulant for your body to get through the afternoon when you will naturally be more tired. Even if you can't get outside, try to avoid having lunch in the same space where you work.
1:00pm - 2:30pm	This is a good time for administrative tasks like team meetings, preparing status updates for clients, and scheduling time for the next day. Time in this block is also well used to catch-up with co-workers as well as relationship building with colleagues and clients.
2:30pm	Take a short break. This break is a good time to socialize with colleagues and go grab a coffee/snack.
2:45pm - 3:15pm	This is a good time for more creative work. Your mind may start to wander but that may be needed for brainstorming or coming up with new ideas/innovations.
3:15pm - 5:00pm	This is a good time for administrative tasks like checking emails, team meetings, preparing status updates for clients, and scheduling time for the next day. Time in this block is also well used to catch-up with co-workers as well as relationship building with colleagues and clients.
5:00pm - 6:00pm	Time to transition between professional and non-professional commitments is an important part of each day. Make sure to take the time you need to refill your tank to give your best to what is most important to you in your personal life.

6:00pm - 7:00pm	This is the best time of day for strength training exercises or to practice yoga for relaxation and flexibility.
7:00pm - 9:00pm	This is a great time for low impact socializing with friends or spending time with family. It is a good time for creative play.
9:00pm - 9:30pm	Start to unplug and keep things low key before bed.
9:30pm - 10:45pm	*Sleep Onset*

SAMPLE AFTERNOON SCHEDULE

Below is an example of the schedule of someone with an Afternoon Pacer.
The times highlighted in gray are the peak performance times for Afternoon
Pacers and the non-highlighted blocks are your non-peak hours. Time
blocking is best done in 60 to 90 minute blocks to align with ultradian cycles.

7:00am - 8:30am	*Wakeup*
Wakeup - 9:00am	Take a few moments to ease into your day. Start your morning with a few deep breaths to improve blood flow and give you a small burst of energy. Eat a protein-rich breakfast. Open the curtains and get a little natural light, this will signal to your body that it is time to start the day.
9:00am - 10:00am	Transition to the workday. Start the morning with administrative tasks like checking email or planning for your day.
10:00am - 11:30am	This is a great time for analytical or strategic tasks. Try to ensure any meetings/calls you take during this time block are ones where you are actively involved in thinking through processes or making decisions, and are not just status updates.
11:30am	Take a short break before transitioning to another focused block. Step away from your computer screen and take a few deep breaths to improve blood flow.
11:45am - 12:30pm	You are likely in your flow during this period. Continue to prioritize tasks that require deep-focus and problem-solving.

12:30pm - 1:30pm	Take a lunch break. This time may also be good for exercise. You are still in your peak focus time so lunch with colleagues or clients may be more fruitful. However you choose to spend the time, make sure that you are allowing at least a few minutes for your mind to have a break.
1:30pm - 3:00pm	Use the last block of your peak time for strategy development or key decision-making.
3:00pm	Take a short break. Grab a coffee or snack to help give you the energy to tackle the rest of the afternoon.
3:15pm - 4:30pm	This is a good time for more creative work. Your mind may start to wander but that may be needed for brainstorming or coming up with new ideas/innovations.
4:30pm	Take a short break away from your computer screen. Taking a few deep breaks will improve blood flow and increase your energy levels.
4:45pm - 6:00pm	This is a good time for administrative tasks like team meetings, preparing status updates for clients, and scheduling time for the next day. Time in this block is also well used to catch-up with co-workers as well as relationship building with colleagues and clients.
6:00pm - 7:00pm	Time to transition between professional and non-professional commitments is an important part of each day. Make sure to take the time you need to refill your tank to give your best to what is most important to you in your personal life.
7:00pm - 9:30pm	This is a great time for low impact socializing with friends or spending time with family. It is a good time for creative play.

9:30pm - 10:30pm	Start to unplug and keep things low key before bed.
10:45pm - 12:00am	*Sleep Onset*

SAMPLE EVENING SCHEDULE

Below is an example of the schedule of someone with an Evening Pacer. The times highlighted in gray are the peak performance times for Evening Pacers and the non-highlighted blocks are your non-peak hours. Time blocking is best done in 60 to 90 minute blocks to align with ultradian cycles. For Evening Pacers more frequent breaks may be necessary for optimal workday pacing. t

8:30am - 9:30am	*Wakeup*
Wakeup - 10:00am	Take a few moments to ease into your day. Start your morning with a few deep breaths to improve blood flow and give you a small burst of energy. Eat a protein-rich breakfast. Open the curtains and get a little natural light, as this will signal to your body that it is time to start the day.
10:00am - 11:00am	Transition to the workday. Start the morning with administrative tasks like checking email or planning for your day. This block will also be a good time for team meetings and preparing status updates for clients.
11:00am	Take a short break before transitioning to another task. Step away from your computer screen and take a few deep breaths to improve blood flow and increase energy.
11:45am - 12:30pm	This is a good time for more creative work. Your mind may start to wander but that may be needed for brainstorming or coming up with new ideas/innovations.
12:30pm	Take a short walk and grab a coffee or snack. If you can get outside and get a little sun it may be a good stimulant for your body to get through the afternoon.

12:45pm - 1:30pm	Continue working on creative tasks. Time in this block is also well used to catch-up with co-workers as well as relationship building with colleagues and clients.
1:30pm - 2:00pm	Take a lunch break or use this block to give yourself a mental break. Consider meditation to let refocus your mind or a quick nap to improve alertness. Consider a shortened lunch break (30 minutes) to allow yourself more frequent short breaks throughout the day.
2:00pm - 3:00pm	Use this time to come up with new ideas, brainstorming alone or with colleagues would be a good use of this block. Time in this block is also well used to catch-up with co-workers and relationship building with clients.
3:00pm	Grab a coffee or a snack to give you the energy you need to get through the afternoon. This break may also be a good time to socialize with colleagues.
3:15pm-4:00pm	This is a good time for tasks like preparing status updates for clients and scheduling time for the next day.
4:00pm	Take a short break away from your computer screen. Taking a few deep breaks will improve blood flow and increase your energy levels.
4:00pm-5:30pm	Begin your focused work. Try to ensure that any meetings/calls that you take during this period are ones where you are actively involved in thinking through processes or making decisions, not just status updates.
5:30pm	Take a short break before transitioning to another focused block.

5:30pm-7:00pm	You are likely in your flow during this period. Continue to work on more analytical tasks or tasks that require more of your focused attention.
7:00pm	Give your mind time to unwind as you transition between professional and non-professional commitments.
7:30pm-9:00pm	This may be an ideal time to practice a focused hobby, spend focused time with friends or family, or to do your most critical work for the day. Use your focused energies to contribute to the people or things most important to you.
8:30pm-9:30pm	This is a good block for yoga or other exercises to increase flexibility.
9:30pm-11:00pm	Consider using this time for problem-solving tasks or making difficult decisions
11:00pm - 12:45am	Start to unplug and keep things low key before bed.
12:45am - 3:00am	*Sleep Onset*

ACKNOWLEDGMENTS

- Caitie Butler - thank you for being the driving force behind this book. It's because of you that we went from idea to actually writing it! Thank you for embracing and developing these concepts, for your skill with words, your project management, and your friendship. (And for letting me use the oxford comma in here!) I am *so* grateful for you!

- Andy - thank you for being my partner and friend, and an undercover MatchPace team member! You've helped me develop frameworks, refine proposals, clarify my thinking, solve thorny problems, and stay the course! You've held me up when I wanted to quit and believe in what I'm doing even when I question it. I'm so glad I married you!

- Nicole Steward Streng - thank you for knowing what MatchPace needed before I ever thought of it! You bring rigor and thoughtfulness to our team, plus kindness and a sense of humor! You help our team grow in so many ways - it's an honor to work with you, and to have you as a friend!

- Steven Kenney - you were one of my first teachers as a consultant, and I continue to learn from your thoughtfulness, work ethic, and deep understanding of how to serve clients. Thank you for believing in MatchPace - I feel so fortunate that you bring your skills to MatchPace and that we get to work together!

- MatchPace Teammates - SMK, KP, LT, VV, RW - thank you for how you contributed your strengths to help MatchPace grow. I'm thankful for each of you and how you helped refine how we serve our clients.

- A big thank you to early MatchPace Clients (and if you're reading this and have already been a client - I'm talking to you!). Thanks for entrusting MatchPace to bring a new perspective to your organization (and letting us test these ideas out on you!)

- Thank you again to my Mom, my Dad, as well as my mother-in-law Peggy - for your overall support of me (there's no way I can thank the three of you enough), enthusiasm for MatchPace, and free childcare!

- Thank you to the professionals who helped bring the book out into the world - Alyssa Miller at Real Eyes Editing; Joy Eggerichs Reed, Holly Bray, Amelia Graves, and Scott James at Punchline Agency; Monica Austin at Mocah Studio. You each brought a unique perspective and skillset that made this possible.

- Thank you to Carly, Danelle, Lucan, Kavitha, Heather, Lisa, Kae, Jen, Lyn, and Gayle. I'm so fortunate to have you all supporting me and MatchPace as professionals and/or friends - you've been sounding boards, advisors, and cheerleaders! And of course thank you to Sarah and Laura for helping me understand the importance of pace, and all the Maxwell women for your friendship!

- The EDJE Team - my children. Thank you for teaching me how to be a better human, for reminding me to be present in the moment, thank you for your patience as I learn how to be a mother, and for your enthusiasm for me as I share my professional skills and gifts through MatchPace.

REFERENCES

[1]"How Many Productive Hours in a Workday?" VoucherCloud, January 2021, https://www.vouchercloud.com/resources/office-worker-productivity

[2]Sarah Green Carmichael, "The Research Is Clear: Long Hours Backfire for People and Companies,"*Harvard Business Review*, August 19, 2015, https://hbr.org/2015/08/the-research-is-clear-long-hours-backfire-for-people-and-for-companies

[3] Pattison, "Worker, Interrupted: The Cost of Task Switching." Fast Company, July 2008.

[4]"Here's Your Brain on Task Switching," MatchPace, August 18, 2020, https://www.matchpace.net/blog/2017/8/28/heres-your-brain-on-task-switching

[5]Jon Staff & Pete Davis, *How to Getaway*, New York: Ramble Press, 2019.

[6]Ben Wigert & Sangeeta Agrawal, "Employee Burnout, Part 1: The 5 Main Causes,"

[7]Lydia Saad, "The "40-Hour" Workweek Is Actually Longer–by Seven Hours," *Gallup*, August 29, 2014, https://news.gallup.com/poll/175286/hour-workweek-actually-longer-seven-hours.aspx

[8]Cal Newport, *Deep Work*, New York: Grand Central Publishing, 2016.

[9]s.v. Burnout, "International Classification of Diseases," *World Health Organization*, www.who.int/standards/classifications/classification-of-diseases

[10]Christina Maslach & Michael P. Leiter, Understanding the burnout experience: recent research and its implications for psychiatry, *World Psychiatry*, June 5, 2016, https://onlinelibrary.wiley.com/doi/full/10.1002/wps.20311

[11]ibid

[12]Gallup, *Employee Burnout: Causes and Cures,* https://www.gallup.com/workplace/282659/employee-burnout-perspective-paper.aspx

[13]Sarah Green Carmichael, "The Research Is Clear: Long Hours Backfire for People and Companies," *Harvard Business Review,* August 19, 2015, https://hbr.org/2015/08/the-research-is-clear-long-hours-backfire-for-people-and-for-companies

[14]Kermit Patteson, "Worker, Interrupted: The Cost of Task Switching," *Fast Company,* July 2008,

[15]Erin Reid, "Why Some Men Pretend to Work 80-Hour Weeks," *Harvard Business Review,* April 28, 2015, https://hbr.org/2015/04/why-some-men-pretend-to-work-80-hour-weeks

[16]Sarah Green Carmichael, "Working Long Hours Makes Us Drink More," *Harvard Business Review,* April 10, 2015, https://hbr.org/2015/04/working-long-hours-makes-us-drink-more

[17]Moshe Sharabi and Itzhak Harpaz, "Core and Peripheral Values: An Overtime Analysis of Work Values in Israel," *Journal of Human Values,* (May 26, 2010), *https://journals.sagepub.com/doi/abs/10.1177/097168581001500206*

[18]Rosie Perper, "Microsoft Japan Trialed a 4-day Workweek", *Business Insider,* November 4, 2019 https://www.businessinsider.com/microsoft-japan-4-day-workweek-40-percent-increase-in-productivity-2019-11

[19]"Flexible Work Schedules," Policy, Data, Oversight, OPM.gov, retrieved January 2021, https://www.opm.gov/policy-data-oversight/pay-leave/work-schedules/fact-sheets/alternative-flexible-work-schedules/

[20]Nicholas Bloom, "Don't Let Employees Pick Their WFH Days," *Harvard Business Review,* May 2021, *https://hbr.org/2021/05/dont-let-employees-pick-their-wfh-days*

[21]ChronoPace scores are informed by the Center for Environmental Therapeutics Morningness/Eveningness Questionnaire Self Assessment (MEQ-SA). Used with License. Purchased 2018.

[22]Chris R. Abyss and Paul B. Laursen, "Describing and Understanding Pacing Strategies during Athletic Competition," *Sports Medicine* 38: 239–252 (2008), *https://link.springer.com/article/10.2165/00007256-200838030-00004*

[23]Susan L. Murphy and Anna L. Kratz, "Activity pacing in daily life: A within-day analysis," *Pain* 155:12, 2630 - 2637, https://www.sciencedirect.com/science/article/abs/pii/S0304395914004515

[24]"Gender Pay Gap Statistics," Payscale, January 2021, https://www.payscale.com/data/gender-pay-gap

[25] "The Wealth Gap and the Race Between Stocks and Homes," Federal Reserve Bank of Minneapolis, July 31, 2018, https://www.minneapolisfed.org/article/2018/the-wealth-gap-and-the-race-between-stocks-and-homes

[26]"Sickness, Disability, and Work: Breaking the Barriers," Organization for Economic Cooperation and Development, November 24, 2010, https://read.oecd-ilibrary.org/social-issues-migration-health/sickness-disability-and-work-breaking-the-barriers_9789264088856-en

[27]Crenshaw, Kimberle, "Demarginalizing the Intersection of Race and Sex: A Black Feminist Critique of Antidiscrimination Doctrine, Feminist Theory and Antiracist Politics," *University of Chicago Legal Forum* 1989: Iss. 1, Article 8. http://chicagounbound.uchicago.edu/uclf/vol1989/iss1/8

[28]Rocío Lorenzo, Nicole Voigt, Miki Tsusaka, Matt Krentz, and Katie Abouzahr, "How Diverse Leadership Teams Boost Innovation," *BCG Henderson Institute*, January 23, 2018, https://www.bcg.com/publications/2018/how-diverse-leadership-teams-boost-innovation

ABOUT THE AUTHORS

Elizabeth Knox is the founder of MatchPace, an organizational effectiveness company that helps teams work well and live well. She empowers teams to work effectively by helping them learn how to create space for collaboration and synergy and to minimize the mess of a typical workday so they can do the deep work that supports the mission of the organization AND ensure people have time for their other priorities.

Elizabeth writes, speaks, consults, and coaches on the importance of working in a way that prioritizes humanity. Her writing has been featured in HuffPost, Thrive Global, and Today's Parents. Her first book, Faith Powered Profession: A Woman's Guide to Living with Faith and Values in the Workplace was published in 2013 and helps women grasp the importance and power of their professional work.

Elizabeth lives in Washington, DC with her husband and four elementary school-aged children.

Caitie Butler loves helping organizations work better and communicate better. After starting her career in politics, she caught Elizabeth's vision for helping organizations work better and joined MatchPace in 2016, now serving as Communications Director. Caitie enjoys writing almost as much as she enjoys reading. She lives with her husband and two young daughters in Helena, MT.